Praise for *Old Paths, ...*

As we pray, God is making us spiritually fit to receive wh[...]
great dreams for what you long to see God do . . . if you [...]
to grow those you lead in their commitment to "praying [...]
Power by my friend Daniel Henderson.

JAMES MACDONALD
Senior Pastor of Harvest Bible Chapel, author of *Act Like Men* and *Vertical Church*

Thank you, Daniel, for calling us back to the centerpiece of all ministry—prayer and the ministry
of the Word of God. As busy pastors, we can be distracted by many good things and incrementally
drawn away from this core calling. We then reap a harvest of ineffectiveness, frustration, and spiritual mediocrity. *Old Paths, New Power* is a timely warning to choose that which God blesses and to
order our lives and ministries around that which produces eternal results.

CRAWFORD W. LORITTS JR.
Author, speaker, radio host, and senior pastor of Fellowship Bible Church, Roswell, GA

Daniel Henderson is one of the finest teachers I know. When he teaches on prayer he is unparal-
leled. In this masterful new volume, he invests all of the prayer treasure he has collected over a
lifetime. When you finish reading it, you will eagerly get on your knees, and vow to never pray
carelessly, casually, or complacently again.

RICHARD BLACKABY
President of Blackaby Ministries International, coauthor of *Experiencing God*

I have firsthand knowledge of the impact of Daniel Henderson's life and ministry. I am his suc-
cessor, which has afforded me the "gift" of building upon his passion for prayer and the ministry
of the Word in the local church. Daniel's ministry, as demonstrated in this book, builds spiritual
depth and maturity into God's people by teaching and modeling for them "how" to worship, pray,
and rely on Christ *alone* for everything.

TROY DOBBS
Senior Pastor, Grace Church, Eden Prairie, MN

Unlike many books on church growth strategy, Daniel Henderson points out the importance
of making the "the next new thing" the "first old thing." This is a must-read book for seminary
professors, seminary students, pastors, ministry leaders, and pastoral search committee members. I
wish this book was written thirty years ago so I could have read it before my first pastorate!

BENNY WONG
Senior Pastor, First Chinese Baptist Church, Los Angeles, CA

When I teach on the personal spiritual disciplines found in Scripture, I always emphasize that the
two most important are the intake of the Word of God and prayer. If a Christian isn't committed to
these, then forget fasting, journaling, and the rest of the disciplines. All other personal spiritual disciplines grow out of and are built on the foundation of the intake of Scripture and prayer. I am grateful
for this valuable resource that reinforces the preeminence of these disciplines above all others.

DONALD S. WHITNEY
Professor of Biblical Spirituality at The Southern Baptist Theological Seminary, author of *Spiritual
Disciplines for the Christian Life*

When it comes to prayer, Daniel Henderson is passionate, personal, and practical. Look at his life
and listen to his words and you just want to pray more and better. He not only calls Christians,
pastors, and churches to prayer but he shows us how to do it.

LEITH ANDERSON
President, National Association of Evangelicals, Washington, DC

Daniel Henderson is the clearest voice on pastor-led prayer and spiritual awakening alive today. *Old Paths, New Power* provides a winsome blueprint to create a thriving culture of prayer and spiritual renewal. Packed with ready-to-use resources, pastors are going to love this book!

BYRON PAULUS
President/Executive Director, Life Action Ministries

I am thankful that the Lord has awakened my heart in recent years with a fresh passion for prayer in my life and within our congregation. In God's providence, we invited Daniel Henderson to come alongside our leadership teams to provide high-impact training for developing and maintaining a dynamic culture of prayer. The principles in this book have changed our staff and I believe they will spark a new Spirit-empowered beginning for you and your ministry.

LON SOLOMON
Senior Pastor, McLean Bible Church, McLean, VA

Daniel Henderson is a trusted voice in directing leadership back to the priority of prayer according to the authority of Scripture. I have greatly benefited from his ministry and have watched his influence shape a culture of prayer on our campus. I highly recommend this work.

JOE KELLER
Vice President of Student Life, The Master's College, Santa Clarita, CA

I also share the vision of Daniel Henderson, and can only imagine what this world would be if God would favor us with an outpouring of his Holy Spirit as practically described in *Old Paths, New Power*. I have dreamed of such, and as a "Pastor to Pastors" for nearly three decades, I know our wildest imaginations can only be realized when the world's clergy are willing to pay God's asking price.

H. B. LONDON
"AMERICA'S Pastor to Pastors"

God calls us to make more and better disciples. The faithful and fruitful pursuit of this call demands a passionate commitment to prayer and the Word (Acts 6:4). Daniel Henderson gets it. This book reveals it. Read and learn from a humble, godly man whose Scripture-fed, Spirit-led, worship-based approach to prayer God has used to transform my prayer life.

WILLIAM WARREN
President, The Mid-Atlantic Baptist Network
Senior Pastor, Allen Memorial Baptist Church, Salisbury, MD

Daniel's prophetic call to return to the old paths is a timely word for all of us who lead in the church. I believe this book will become a catalyst in the lives of pastors to start chasing after God and the power that can only come through prayer.

LANCE WITT
President and founder of Replenish Ministries

The principles in this book have helped me as a senior pastor to deepen my personal experience in prayer, as well as lead our congregation in moving from being a church that prays to becoming a praying church. As a result, Acts 6:4 is no longer just a text I teach, but an experience I regularly enjoy.

DANNY HODGES
Senior Pastor, Calvary Chapel, St. Petersburg, FL

DANIEL HENDERSON

OLD PATHS NEW POWER

*Awakening Your Church through Prayer
and the Ministry of the Word*

MOODY PUBLISHERS
CHICAGO

Edited by Jim Vincent
Interior design: Erik M. Peterson
Cover design: Dean Renninger
Cover image of rock cave copyright © by Dawson / Lightstock (238605). All rights reserved.
Author photo credit: Kelly Weaver Photography

Library of Congress Cataloging-in-Publication Data

Names: Henderson, Daniel, author.
Title: Old paths, new power : awakening your church through prayer and the ministry of the word / by Daniel Henderson.
Description: Chicago : Moody Publishers, 2016. | Includes bibliographical references.
Identifiers: LCCN 2016011941 (print) | LCCN 2016012881 (ebook) | ISBN 9780802414465 | ISBN 9780802494061 ()
Subjects: LCSH: Church renewal. | Prayer--Christianity. | Preaching. | Revivals.
Classification: LCC BV600.3 .H449 2016 (print) | LCC BV600.3 (ebook) | DDC 269--dc23
LC record available at http://lccn.loc.gov/2016011941

We hope you enjoy this book from Moody Publishers. Our goal is to provide high-quality, thought-provoking books and products that connect truth to your real needs and challenges. For more information on other books and products written and produced from a biblical perspective, go to www.moodypublishers.com or write to:

Moody Publishers
820 N. LaSalle Boulevard
Chicago, IL 60610

3 5 7 9 10 8 6 4 2

Printed in the United States of America

Contents

Foreword

I am honored to write this foreword to *Old Paths, New Power* because I have personally benefited from what Daniel Henderson has written about prayer and from his personal passion and example. For almost a decade he has led the early-morning prayer sessions at the Moody Bible Institute's Pastors Conference. Hundreds of pastors attend these early-morning sessions with hungry hearts and high expectations. They are rewarded with a fresh approach to praying, worshiping, and connecting with each other.

Long ago I learned that the reason so many Christians do not attend prayer meetings is because they have found them—forgive me for saying it—*boring*. They pray about the same old things in the same old way. Daniel's approach is life-giving to our souls. He leads us with Scripture-fed, Spirit-led, worship-based prayers, and in the process he models how we as pastors can lead our own prayer meetings with anticipation and creativity.

My prayer is that this book will be used by the Lord to bring prayer back into our families and churches. My observation is that the evangelical church does a great deal of complaining about the demise of our culture, the low level of political discourse, and the encroaching religious darkness. Helpless as we are to stem these ominous tides, yet incredibly we still do not humble ourselves and pray. We lament that we have not seen a revival, but we are not yet desperate enough to seek God for such an outpouring.

In *Old Paths, New Power* Daniel articulates his passion with rich biblical insight and practical applications. These are the vital and urgent lessons most of us never learned in seminary. Yet they are truths we must learn and apply if we are going to have pastoral impact that is both biblical and supernatural.

Daniel's insights have been forged by decades of relentless attention to the priority of prayer in pastoral ministry. He would be the first to admit that he has not arrived in his prayer leadership, but he issues a clear, compelling call to every pastor to join him in pursuit of the New Testament ideal of "prayer and the ministry of the word" (Acts 6:4 NIV). This is the theme of The 6:4 Fellowship, an organization Daniel leads, dedicated to helping pastors live out Acts 6:4 in churches across America.

If you are a layman in your church, purchase a copy of this book for your pastor. I believe any pastor authentically interested in a work of revival will be encouraged, enlightened, and empowered by the timely and timeless principles of *Old Paths, New Power*.

I enthusiastically commend this book to you and look forward to countless Christ-exalting reports of churches that are experiencing profound progress toward becoming a "house of prayer for all nations."

ERWIN LUTZER
Pastor Emeritus, Moody Church, Chicago

Preface

Daniel Henderson helped me to pray out of the Word of God early in my ministry. We would meet in the morning, open our Bible, and pray Scripture truths. Over the years I've continued to set that example in our church services as I read the Scripture and pray from that passage, showing our people how to pray from the Bible. As a result, prayer has become a dynamic reality in our church. This is part of the pastor's pursuit of the balance of "prayer and the ministry of the word."

At a personal level, my most intense times of prayer are the hours when I am in the Word of God. Studying and teaching the Bible is my life. I spend most of my ministry effort studying the Word of God, and I can't hear God without concentrated prayer. Those are the richest times of prayer for me.

Unfortunately in today's climate, many pastors feel too busy for these priorities. The "ministry of the word" has become shallow and prayer has become superficial. I believe the pastorate is one profession where men are most confused about what they are supposed to do. Many pastors think they are to function as some kind of middle manager or a broker of chosen theologies. However, the foundation of what they are to do is "prayer and ministry of the word," even as the early church leaders did, according to Acts 6:4.

In *Old Paths, New Power*, Daniel explores this biblical pattern and applies it to our day, showing us how, through prayer and devotion to the Scriptures, we can change our church and our world. Writing from his years of experience and deep biblical conviction, he gives pastors a clear and practical pathway for returning to the original description of pastoral ministry. Just as Daniel helped me many years ago, I believe he will give you fresh understanding, resolve, and clarity about God's call for every pastor.

JOHN MACARTHUR
Pastor-Teacher, Grace Community Church,
Sun Valley, California

Now in these days when the disciples were increasing in number, a complaint by the Hellenists arose against the Hebrews because their widows were being neglected in the daily distribution. And the twelve summoned the full number of the disciples and said, "It is not right that we should give up preaching the word of God to serve tables. Therefore, brothers, pick out from among you seven men of good repute, full of the Spirit and of wisdom, whom we will appoint to this duty. *But we will devote ourselves to prayer and to the ministry of the word.*" And what they said pleased the whole gathering, and they chose Stephen, a man full of faith and of the Holy Spirit, and Philip, and Prochorus, and Nicanor, and Timon, and Parmenas, and Nicolaus, a proselyte of Antioch. These they set before the apostles, and they prayed and laid their hands on them.
And the word of God continued to increase, and the number of the disciples multiplied greatly in Jerusalem, and a great many of the priests became obedient to the faith.

ACTS 6:1–7 (emphasis added)

The key to a new movement of the
Spirit of God will not be in a new
technique, but in the "old" paths of
Gospel proclamation, earnest prayer,
and yearning for the Spirit.[1]

J. D. GREEAR

———————————

The church always goes forward
best by going back first.[2]

OS GUINNESS

Introduction

Imagine!

Imagine sitting down one morning at the kitchen table, coffee in hand. You open the local paper with little anticipation, except to discover more depressing stories about economic woes, international conflict, crimes of various varieties, and more political punditry. Suddenly, a riveting headline arrests your attention:

CHURCHES ACROSS USA GROW RAPIDLY, LEADERS CANNOT EXPLAIN WHY

With curiosity on high alert, you grab your smartphone and begin to search for similar stories. Unexpectedly, the news reports leap off the screen. You can't believe what you are seeing. You have prayed for this, although not always in faith. You have longed for this kind of breakthrough in your own church, wondering if it would ever come. Then you recall that in recent days you have seen an unusual uptick in prayer and fresh stirrings of the Spirit in your own congregation . . . and pondered. But now your Google search takes you to more headlines:

From Miami:	**Five Rabbis Leave their Synagogues For Christian Church after Dramatic Conversion**
From Greater Minneapolis:	**Dozens of Islamic Leaders Renounce Their Faith to Join Christian Movement**

From Orange County, Calif.:	**Local Buddhist Priests Cause Stir by Declaring that Jesus Christ Is God**
From Salt Lake City:	**Mormon Leaders to Discard Extrabiblical Documents in Dramatic Shift of Core Beliefs**
From New England:	**Recent Surveys Show Bible Sales up 200%**
From *Time* magazine:	**Leading Atheists Embrace Evidence for Jesus' Resurrection, Offer Public Apologies to Christians**

Your excitement rises in inexpressible gratitude and profound new expectation. The great hope of Jesus Christ living through a revived church seems to be dawning with entirely unanticipated developments. The prayers of God's people over decades of desperate intercession are now coming to fruition, redeeming opponents of the Gospel and transforming communities across the landscape.

And it has come just in time. Everything in the news in recent years has pointed to a dramatic downturn in the spiritual influence of the church. The cultural indicators have screamed a thunderous warning that America is in a rapid post-Christian spiral. Believers have actually been labeled as the obstructionists in a secular society, a society defined by tolerance toward everything, except absolute truth.

As you read these reports you cannot escape the thought that revival has finally arrived. The sparks have kindled in small places where people have been praying. As a midwife carefully guides new life into the world, it seems that pastors have lovingly labored for this day, true to the calling to make each of their churches a "house of prayer for all nations."

You have read about the Great Awakenings and their impact on society in previous centuries. Could this be the inauguration of a similar work of the Spirit? The evidence is undeniable. Organic

14

awakenings are birthing in hearts, congregations, and communities. What might this mean to the church in the future? What role should you play in this fresh work of the Word and Spirit?

COULD IT HAPPEN?

Having roused your imagination with this hopeful possibility, let me ask, "Could a moment like this happen in our lifetime?" I would propose that it could indeed. Not only has it happened in our not-so-distant history, but such a far-reaching revival of this kind of transforming Gospel impact is recorded in the New Testament.

Fascination grips me as I ponder what I believe is the greatest "revival" moment in the New Testament narrative. Transcending a difficult environment, one that would soon go from tough to tougher, the early Christ followers form a fearless Gospel community empowered in the greater reality of Jesus Christ, prayer, and the Holy Spirit. In Acts 6:7 we read these words: "And the word of God continued to increase, and the number of the disciples multiplied greatly in Jerusalem, and a great many of the priests became obedient to the faith."

Read that again slowly. Try to absorb the profound and practical implications of what is being said. Think about the incalculable impact described in this one succinct sentence. Remember that for the first five chapters in the book of Acts, thousands were being "added" to the church in Jerusalem. By Acts 6:1, the numbers were multiplying. Some scholars believe the church could have had as many as twenty thousand men and women as chapter 6 commences.[3] But by verse 7 it says that the number of Gospel-transformed lives had "multiplied greatly." Put away the calculator. The numbers were officially off the chart. The Spirit was on the move. The Gospel was going viral.

But don't miss this astounding observation: A "great many of the priests" were being converted (v. 7). These Jewish priests were hard-liners, tough opponents of the gospel. The network of religious rivals who conspired to crucify Christ was now losing a significant number of its own ranks to a transformation found in the life of the resurrected Jesus. It would be like a modern-day salvation wave that engulfs some of the most notable atheists and critics of the faith in our day. Truly amazing. Truly God. Truly the way the Gospel ought to be.

AWAKENING THE CHURCH

This is a snapshot of what we have come to call a "Great Awakening" in society that transforms the very fabric of the spiritual landscape through the Gospel. Great Awakenings have happened in past centuries, with a holy, sanctifying effect upon churches and individuals. Such change always begins with a revival in the church. "Revival" means to live in a new way. New power springs from the old paths of New Testament life and leadership.

Revival in the church has always been rooted in a personal, organic, heart-to-heart awakening of God's people. To be awakened is to be roused from sleep, to rise from a drowsy state, to become aware for the first time.

God's people are awakened to the sufficiency and supernatural power of the Holy Spirit. They are awakened to hear and apply the Scriptures, the living Word of God, to their lives with ruthless authenticity. They are awakened to the seriousness of sin, leading to a new and powerful repentance. They are awakened to the beauty and blessing of prevailing prayer. They are awakened to the tragic heartbreak of the lost condition of relatives, friends, neighbors, and work associates. In short, they are awakened to Christ—the supremacy of His power, the obligation of His purposes, and the potency of his promises and His indwelling presence to accomplish all of the above. Pastor J. D. Greear has noted:

> In an awakening, the Spirit of God does not typically do a "new" thing; he simply pours greater power upon the "normal" things faithful Christians are already doing. Prayers become more intense; worship becomes more joyous; repentance becomes more sorrowful; and the preached Word yields greater effect. The Spirit of God multiplies the effectiveness of our "normal" work of seed-planting, bringing a bountiful harvest. And he does more in a moment than we can accomplish in a lifetime.[4]

I can't help it. I wake up every day dreaming of this kind of movement again. Looking, longing for those headlines. The passion became so compelling that several years ago I left a secure calling as the senior pastor of a four-thousand-member church, after twenty-five years in pastoral ministry, to give my entire life to this kind of vision. Yet the passion runs deep and the need arises paramount. I want to serve as a spiritual pyromaniac in igniting the heart of the church for Christ's glory. I am privileged to partner with pastors all across the country every year toward this important aspiration.

Do you dream too? Could it happen again? Could it explode in our lifetime? Could you be used of God to help lead the way in a movement of unprecedented proportions to see the Gospel spread like wildfire and countless lives transformed?

SIMPLY SUPERNATURAL

Let me make a vital observation. This kind of revival moment in Acts 6:1 was not the result of some well-planned evangelistic strategy. It occurred without cushy ministry budgets. High profile leaders did not coalesce to sponsor big events to try to change the tide. The early church had no buildings, no organized programs, no technology, no social media, and no superstars who spoke or wrote about recently formulated methodologies for attracting a bigger crowd.

This was not a moment birthed by human enterprise but the fruit of an unmistakable environment. I describe leaders as "environmental specialists." Either God uses them to shape ministry environments that facilitate supernatural results—or those leaders can perpetuate programmatic endeavors without the Spirit.

In this book we want to unpack (hopefully in compelling, clear, and practical terms) the approach of the early apostles, who nurtured and relentlessly preserved an environment of supernatural ministry essence. They maintained primary focus—a focus that they had observed and received directly from Christ. They refused to get distracted with lesser priorities. As a mother bear protects her cubs, they guarded core commitments that facilitated *a supernatural work of the Spirit.* They were not to be diverted, derailed, diluted, or discouraged. This was their Acts 6:4 focus: to commit their best and most substantive leadership energies "to prayer and to the ministry of the word," while empowering other Spirit-filled leaders to take on critical responsibilities. This sets the stage for a revival.

I know some might read this and dismiss it as an old-school paradigm that is only relevant for monks meandering in the isolation of a monastery. Others could reject it as a simplistic, even naive approach that is inadequate for our highly sophisticated, technically dependent, and super complex ministry environment of the twenty-first century. Some will find it dull while even more could feel disinterest based on previously failed experiences in pursuing a meaningful work of renewal.

I am hoping and praying that you sense a stirring—a deep craving that says "I'm in." Maybe you are like me, and thousands of ministry influencers I interact with every year, who are tired of the next new formula spoonfed to us by celebrity pastors. Maybe your heart is feeling a compulsion, as mine has, that the "next new thing" must be "the first old thing."

SUPPLEMENT OR SUBSTANCE?

The apostolic Acts 6:4 tenacity was not a supplement to the crafting of the apostles' ministry plans. *It was the essential lifeline for receiving Christ's direction and provision.* It was not an ambitious strategy to grow a bigger church. Rather, it was the life-giving environment to grow healthy, spiritually passionate disciples, starting with their own hearts. They recognized that leading the church was a supernatural assignment, not a ministry enterprise. They could not afford to move away from a full and focused experience of Christ's person and presence to solve operational problems or implement a new program. Even when the pressing need of the moment held the potential of significant disruption and division, like the breakdown of the important widow-feeding program, they were resolute.

Today's pastors face pressing dilemmas that can easily derail spiritual focus. Trying to breathe life into dying programs or driving the creation of new initiatives can consume every ounce of energy of the pastoral team. It is never too soon to ask how much time the church leadership teams are actually devoting to prayer and the ministry of the Word, like the early apostles. Their commitment ushered in a powerful new work of the Spirit. Our priorities must be scrutinized and evaluated as to the real eternally significant impact they are producing.

These early church leaders knew that ministry was received, not achieved. Their understanding was not that they had to reach the world for Christ but that Christ was ready to reach the world through them. The first depends largely on human effort, talent, strategy, and programming. The other is experienced through the power of the living Christ and indwelling Spirit working super-naturally in accordance with the Scripture. It is enacted for the glory of God alone, by advancing the Gospel.

Prayer was not an escape from the thorny predicaments of ministry. Prayer was an engagement with the One who alone had the wisdom, direction, power, and unifying grace to enable the apostles to address these concerns as opportunities—opportunities for Christ's glory, as they manifested His strength through their human weaknesses.

FROM A MINISTRY
CONTEXT TO A PRAYER CONTEXT

My friend and fellow pastor Keeney Dickenson notes, "We pray in the context of ministry, but Jesus ministered in the context of prayer."[5] These apostles had seen, felt, and been changed forever by how Christ lived, taught, and implemented the gospel ministry. They were imitating the One who did only what He saw His Father doing, and who lived in this zone of spiritual insight and power every day, through His life of prayer. They dared not create a different paradigm. They had to walk in His steps through prayer and the ministry of the Word.

Certainly this is no easy task in our highly driven, results-oriented, technologically savvy world. The average pastor's calendar includes meetings to attend, staff problems to untangle, visits to make, services to plan, board meetings to navigate, programs to tweak, and a family to shepherd in the midst of it all. Yet, it can be done. It must be done. Too much is at stake to presume on or neglect the still-relevant outcomes of "prayer and the ministry of the word." Any revival is founded on fervent prayer. (See John Dickerson's passionate call to revival in "On the Path to Power" at the end of this introduction.)

A REDISCOVERED FAITH

I have heard it said that "if you are excited about what God is doing elsewhere, don't mimic the miracle, imitate the faith." This book is about rediscovering the faith of the early apostles as they exhibited a world-shaking confidence in the sufficiency of the Spirit of God through prayer, the Word of God through Gospel preaching, and the people of God through trusting empowerment. While the Acts 6 moment is descriptive of these realities, it is clearly the expression of what is abundantly prescriptive in the New Testament and powerfully patterned by Jesus Christ.

The moment is urgent for pastors to find a path for better priorities and greater impact. Because seminary did not prepare most of us to lead a dynamic prayer environment in our churches, this book seeks to give you deeper resolve and proven approaches to facilitate life-giving movements of renewal in your congregation. These are realities I have learned in the "school of hard knocks" through thirty-plus years of pastoral ministry. I've seen thousands of lives transformed. Countless pastors are returning to the old paths to embrace these paradigms with dynamic and fruitful results.

Jim Cymbala, pastor of The Brooklyn Tabernacle, notes, "We often must go backward to move forward. If we want to experience sorely needed blessings from God, we must return to the old pathways of seeking God's Spirit and avoid the 'new' that is not ultimately true."

We need an urgent rediscovery of early church leadership and a return to New Testament power. In this moment it's apparent that the American church is drifting. All indicators would also point to an impending sifting. There has not been a more critical moment in recent history. It is a moment that calls us to the core supernatural realities of ministry. This is our only hope and must be our clarion conviction. It is time for a necessary, indescribable awakening among God's people—starting with the ones sitting in your services every weekend.

ON THE PATH TO POWER

Revival or Recession?
BY JOHN S. DICKERSON

You should hear their prayers, as they kneel, crying out to God through tears. These are the desperate prayers we expect to hear from believers hiding underground in Asia, from those bearing the scars of Christ on their flesh in Syria and Afghanistan.

And yet I am witnessing God's servant-leaders crying such prayers here in the United States. I am describing hundreds of American Christian pastors and servant-leaders physically on their knees before God, confessing their pride, confessing a dependence on human priorities rather than on heaven's.

I have witnessed this moment among leaders from multiple denominations, churches of all sizes, and nationally known parachurch ministries. I have heard this corporate submission before God in Dallas, Nashville, Jacksonville, Indianapolis, Chicago, Phoenix, Grand Rapids, and other cities across America.

When we face the facts about cultural change in America, about increasing hostility toward Christians, and our failure to disciple our own children, we realize that we have before us two options in the American church:

(1) Recession, the continued gradual but steady receding of biblical Christianity in the United States; or

(2) Revival, a fresh work of God not engineered or manufactured by human strategists, but unleashed by God's Spirit.

As a journalist with expertise in summarizing boxes of data,[6] I set out a few years ago to take the pulse of Bible-believing Christianity. I did so by aggregating thousands of pages from multiple researchers. The resulting book, *The Great Evangelical Recession*, unveils a mosaic of the church in America.

The data reveals a smaller American church than many of us thought, a movement declining as a percentage of the population, largely failing to disciple its own children, and increasingly oppressed by powerful forces in the broader culture.

The Great Evangelical Recession released in 2013. It predicted that, barring a radical change in trajectory, the church in the U.S. will continue being pushed to the periphery of society, that hostility toward Christians will increase, and that some large ministries will begin struggling financially because they rely on donations from the oldest two generations. Since then we have seen the following:

- The Southern Baptist Convention has announced it will cut 600 to 800 missionary staff, calling missionaries home from the field, due to a $210 million funding shortage.[7]

- An American Christian has been physically jailed for refusing to sign her personal signature on a same-sex marriage license.[8]

- A brilliant tech innovator, inventor of the JavaScript programming language, has been publicly shamed and forced out of the company he cofounded, Mozilla, because of his Christian views.[9]

- The Supreme Court ruled to redefine marriage nationwide, effectively vetoing the "Defense of Marriage Act" and constitutional amendments across many of the 50 United States. The President celebrated by illumining the White House in the symbolic rainbow colors of gay pride.
- *New York Times* columnist Nicholas Kristof, himself not a Christian, described his concern about increasing hatred toward Christians in the leading edges of society, writing "In liberal circles, evangelicals constitute one of the few groups that it's safe to mock openly."[10]

These changes were more or less predicted in 2013 by simple analysis of value trajectories among Americans.

People sometimes ask if I believe the church is faring better or worse, presently, than it was in 2013. My observation is that the hostility toward Christians continues accelerating, far quicker than some insulated Christian leaders realize. The cultural mile markers are clear to anyone looking, and the generational value-changes driving these shifts are increasing with each passing year and with each younger generation.

The leading segments of American society are now deeply infected with anti-Christian sentiment: mainstream media, the influential coastal metropolises, the TV and film industries, Silicon Valley, much of the federal government, and higher academia—which shapes the worldview not only of the emerging generation, but also of the future generations they will teach. (This is not to ignore the exceptional Christians serving in each of these industries. The faithful, increasingly silent believers in these arenas are just that, exceptions.)

Question: *Why is the wealthiest church in world history declining in both size and cultural influence?* I believe the answer lies in this simple statement:

In the midst of these developments, the great strength in the American church has become its greatest weakness.

Somewhere along the way, unintentionally and gradually, we moved our feet of faith away from desperate dependence on the resurrection of Christ, away from the Holy Spirit as our only source of power, away from desperate times of prayer.

We believe these things in our doctrinal statements (and that's good). But we do not believe them in our actions.

Slowly, unintentionally, our feet of faith have shifted away from prayer as the only means of siphoning supernatural strength through the dimensions of the universe, into our human world.

We in the American church have more resources than any other church in history. And, as the gravity of human nature so often tends, our actionable faith has drifted to depend on these tangible resources (dollars, political clout, facilities, paid staffs). There is nothing morally wrong with these tangible resources. But we are witnessing the principle of sowing and reaping.

We have sowed to human ingenuity, strategy, and power. We have sowed through recent decades to the power of new buildings and congressional lobbying. And we are reaping what we sowed.

How do we return to sowing seeds of faith that desperately depend on God's Word, His Spirit, and Himself? Scripture answers this question: "Humble yourselves, therefore, under the mighty hand of God so that at the proper time he may exalt you" (1 Peter 5:6).

Scripture also warns us: "God opposes the proud but gives grace to the humble" (1 Peter 5:5; cf. Prov. 3:34).

We who lead ministries are far too self-groomed to be overtly proud in our speech. It is our actions that reflect our truest, most sinister pride. We proclaim self-dependence rather than God-dependence in our schedules and in our time devoted to human efforts that are un-prayed. Where we are proud we will meet the resistance of heaven. Where we are humble (God dependent), we will find God's grace—as churches in China, Africa, and Syria are experiencing, even in the face of human suffering.

If we will listen, we will hear the marching movement of great, unseen spiritual factions. If we will suspend our thoughts of salary, retirement, self-comfort, we will see that much of the church in the United States has become spiritually anemic and culturally out-matched.

Faced with such facts, we can choose one of three responses:

1. *Ignore the evidence* and continue with business as usual. Continue losing our own young people, declining as a percentage of the population, and failing to be ambassadors who bring Good News to a pagan culture.
2. *Acknowledge the facts but despair* and bemoan our sad state, for lack of faith.
3. *Acknowledge the facts and turn to God* in desperate faith.

I am encouraged to see servant-leaders choosing the third response all across the United States. They are desperately turning to God in prayers of humility, self-abandon, and fresh God-dependence. Like a starving child shoveling food into his mouth with both hands, pastors and leaders are discovering how starved they are for corporate times of sincere extended prayer.

Get them on their knees. Get them praying in repentance and desperation, and they begin leading each other, spiritually, through their prayers. They begin crying. They begin speaking psalms, hymns, and spiritual songs. They begin spurring each other toward love and good deeds. They encounter the old power that got them into this game in the first place.

It does not require a dynamic human leader to launch such a prayer movement, because the dynamic Leader already exists, in the Holy Spirit. God is searching for servants who will be humbly bold enough to invite the Spirit's leadership into times of corporate prayer.

My hope for you, chosen servant of the King, is that this book equips and ignites you to fan into flame such a movement of prayer, beginning in your own closet, then continuing to your staff or disciples, and beyond into other believers.

Together, let us be a movement of believers who humble ourselves before the Lord, who pray as if God's moving is our first hope, our last hope, our only hope.

If the struggles of the American church shake us, awaken us, then they do us good. The hope of the church has never been its cultural footing; the hope of the church has always been the resurrection power of Christ. The power of the church has never been within its measure of people, but always in its measure of the Holy Spirit.

When the apostles were threatened in Acts 5, a Pharisee demonstrated great faith in God's true power. He said of the apostles "if their purpose or activity is of human origin, it will fail. But if it is from God, you will not be able to stop these men" (Acts 5:38–39 NIV).

I wonder if we actually believe Gamaliel's claim about God in our own ministry efforts:

- If my activity is human in origin, it will fail.
- If my activity is from God, nobody will be able to stop it.

When I believe this, I begin seeing prayer as Jesus did—a time of humbly aligning myself with the Father, asking what His purposes for the day are, and aligning myself with the invincible, unstoppable raging redemption of God.

You and I will not give account to God for the entire church in the United States. But we will give account for the flocks we oversee (Hebrews 13). In that flock, do you desire to see gradual receding and reduction, moved along by the currents of the culture? Or do you desire to see supernatural revival, moved along by the breathing, living Spirit of God?

"If my people, who are called by my name, will humble themselves, and pray," then He will hear from heaven (cf. 2 Chron. 7:14 NIV).

John S. Dickerson is author of The Great Evangelical Recession. *Learn more at JohnSDickerson.com.*

PART 1

CHRIST'S SUFFICIENCY IN THE OLD PATHS

Arguably, no time in church history has more closely approximated the first-century beginning of the church than now. Our ancient brethren faced a pagan pre-Christian culture. Similarly, the contemporary church encounters a pagan, post-Christian, and postmodern world. The essential biblical model of ministry of the first century has never been more appropriate than it is today.[1]

RICHARD MAYHEW

Christians in China are praying for our Christian brothers and sisters in America. We believe we are handling our persecution better than you are handling your prosperity.[2]

A CHRISTIAN LEADER IN CHINA

1

Current Drift —
Future Sift

F or every Gospel action, there is an opposite and devious de-
monic reaction. We see this in the book of Acts. It appears in
church history. We experience it in our personal journeys.

The Gospel revolution began when the Spirit empowered the
resurrection witnesses on the day of Pentecost. Thousands were converted, baptized, and enfolded in a matter of hours. In the following days, thousands more would convert. In Acts 6:7 multiplying
masses became a part of the believing assembly of Christ followers.

But Satan did not roll over. He reloaded. In Acts 4, he attacked
via persecution. Peter and John were seized, threatened, and told
to cease their Gospel preaching endeavors (Acts 4:1–22). In chapter 5, the enemy attacked through corruption, motivating Ana-
nias and Sapphira to lie about their giving (Acts 5:1–11). Later
in chapter 5, another wave of persecution struck. This time the
apostles were arrested, threatened, and beaten (Acts 5:17–40).
Then, in Acts 6, a more subtle snare emerged as the enemy sought
to promote division and distraction. Disunion between the Greek
and Hebrew-speaking believers arose over the neglect of the Greek
widows. The apostles were required to address the administrative
breakdown that could lead to breakup (Acts 6:1).

So the Acts 6 spiritual resurgence arose in the midst of relentless spiritual counterattack. As I've noted, this occurred in a religiously hostile environment. Persecution by the Jewish authorities was dogging the apostles at every turn. Prohibitions against preaching the Gospel were enforced. The Jewish leaders had jailed the apostles and would soon launch a movement of martyrdom, starting in chapter 7 with Stephen's death by stoning.

Politically, the government in power when the early church began following Christ's ascension was anything but conservative. It certainly was not faith-friendly. We know that the Roman Empire was ruled by blood-thirsty leaders who were womanizers and commonly married multiple times. Past and present Roman emperors were worshiped as gods, some having their own temples erected in their honor. They touted a society of religious tolerance but would soon lower the hammer on Christians who worshiped only one God and Savior. Quickly Christians became despised and labeled as obstructionists to the prevailing religion and irreligion of the day. In this environment, Christians were branded as antisocial for not participating in the pagan norms of their communities. They were dubbed as contrary to the spiritual atmosphere of the day because they refused to worship the Roman gods.

In time, the Christ followers were classified as dangerous because the prevailing belief was that the "gods" were upset with those who refused to worship pagan style. It was believed that their Christian views were bringing a divine judgment upon the empire.

MORE PRESSURE—MORE POWER

By the end of the second century, the Christian apologist Tertullian complained about this widespread perception. "They think the Christians the cause of every public disaster, of every affliction with which the people are visited. If the Tiber rises as high as the city walls, if the Nile does not send its waters up over the fields, if the heavens give no rain, if there is an earthquake, if there is famine or pestilence, straightway the cry is, 'Away with the Christians to the lions!'"[3]

Nero, who ruled in the second half of the first century, distinguished himself by dipping the martyred bodies of Christians in oil and using them as torches to light his royal courtyards. We've all heard the accounts of his burning Rome, then blaming the Christians to justify blatant persecution that even featured believers in the Coliseum, eaten alive by wild animals before a frenzied crowd.

I believe we could conclude that the revival of Acts 6 was the impetus to the increased persecution. The incredible power of the Gospel became a threat to Judaism of the day and to the larger Roman society. At the same time, this revival served as preparation for the coming oppression, providing supernatural grace, transcendent resolve, and staunch boldness that would turn the world upside down (Acts 17:6).

Without question, we too are in need of a momentous Acts 6 movement of prayer and proclamation of the Word. I also cannot help but wonder if this will be the ultimate preparation for a coming sifting of the church. In all likelihood, a revival will advance the supernatural spread of the Gospel but will also fast-track the inevitable showdown between an intolerant culture and the truth of Jesus Christ.

PRESENT DRIFT

Let's be honest. The spiritual awakening in Acts 6 seems a distant cry from the modern-day environment of church as we know it. And church as we know it is not working.

Ministry as "usual" has become a slow dribble toward our cultural margins. But because we don't like "usual" we've created other labels. Ministry as "innovative" is capturing some attention but ultimately is not advancing the Gospel in a disinterested society. Ministry as "clever" lights up Twitter, but it is eclipsing the glory of Christ. As I often heard Jim Cymbala say, "It is hard for me to be clever and make Jesus beautiful at the same time."

Ministry defined by the latest "formulas" leaves us baffled. We soon discover that wearing someone else's ministry clothes never seems to be a fit. Ministry as "attractional" is gathering larger, less discipled and less missional crowds. Ministry as a showcase for "leadership" is creating some rock stars but not anchoring our souls in the Rock of Ages. Ministry as "denominational" is wavering as we put more energy into religious bureaucracy and research but with few supernatural results.

By New Testament measurements, we are anemic and shallow. We certainly are distracted. Could it be that we are powerless at the very moment when our society needs to experience the reality of faith that rests on the power of God and not the wisdom of men (1 Cor. 2:5)?

In Their Own Words

Watch senior pastor Alistair Begg (Parkside Church, Solon, OH) describe "The State of Pastoral Ministry" at http://www.64fellowship.com/oldpaths/01

In his thought-provoking book, *The Great Evangelical Recession*, John S. Dickerson unpacks a much-needed wake-up call for the American church. Not only does he validate the coming reality of decreased giving and increased cultural hostility to the church, but he gives an accurate assessment of the actual number of evangelicals in the United States today. Based on four different studies, each with unique and verifiable research approaches, Dickerson reports that the number of evangelical Christians is actually between 7 and 9 percent of the US population. This comes as a shock to those of us who believed that the numbers were closer to 40 percent or more.[4] Meanwhile a recent study by the Barna Group finds "the percentage of Americans who qualify as "postChristian" rose by 7 percentage points, from 37 percent in 2013 to 44 percent in 2015. Across the United States, cities in every state are becoming more "postChristian." They summarize, "An increasing number of religiously unaffiliated, a steady drop in church attendance, the recent Supreme Court decision on same-sex marriage, and the growing tension over religious freedoms all point to a larger secularizing trend sweeping across the nation."[5]

The Southern Baptists, the largest evangelical denomination, unveiled troubling news in a recent annual report. Despite adding more churches to the SBC roster, the total number of churches lost more than 200,000 members, the biggest one-year decline since 1881. Membership fell by 1.5 percent, while weekly worship attendance dipped 2.75 percent in the same year. Baptisms fell eight of the last ten years, with last year being the lowest total since 1947.[6] More recently the SBC International Mission Board president David Platt announced that the agency needs to cut at least six hundred missionaries and staff to balance its budget. Those cuts are needed to make up for a $21 million deficit for 2015.[7]

Thom S. Rainer, president of LifeWay, the Southern Baptist's publishing arm, responded, "It breaks my heart that the trend of our denomination is mostly one of decline. Programs and meetings are not going to revive our people—only prayer and repentance will lead our people to revival."[8]

THE FUTURE VIEW

And it is not looking hopeful as we think of what will happen in coming generations. For the most part, the Millennial generation has closed the door on church involvement. Among those who grew up in church, nearly six in ten have dropped out at some point.

Three in ten Millennials say church is not at all important, while an additional four in ten are ambivalent, saying church is either somewhat important or somewhat not important.[9] And it is likely to get worse with the next wave of children being raised by a spiritually disinterested generation. Apart from a different approach to ministry and something truly supernatural, we are in trouble.

Hockey great Wayne Gretzky said, "I always skate to where the puck is going rather than to where it's been." As the church, we need to embrace this. It's not that the puck of the American church is moving ahead like a well-executed sudden-death shootout between the Pittsburgh Penguins and Anaheim Ducks. Rather, the culture is waiting down the road for our arrival, like a disbelieving acquaintance who is unsure of our trustworthiness. But our real need is not to be "relevant" through new self-styled efforts to morph into a more palatable version of faith. Our need is to be revived in the New Testament essence of church leadership that will answer a hostile and wary culture with a display of all that makes Christianity unique and triumphant—the power of the Gospel, lived and proclaimed in supernatural power.

This book is not a call for some new growth strategy to correct the heartrending decline. Rather it is a hopeful call to a renaissance. A reawakening. A resolve to make "the next new thing" the "first old thing." We must discover a new understanding of power in the old paths of New Testament ministry and anticipate a powerful intersection of this reality with a befuddled society.

FUTURE SIFT—NEEDFUL SHIFT

In our present moment we are clearly accelerating in the transition to a postChristian culture. Some would say we are already there—living in a culture hostile to people of faith. The present moment has even been dubbed as a society of "Christophobia."[10]

The sifting has begun and the shifting of our paradigms is approaching. With two thousand years of church history behind us, we have a reliable trail of evidence on the rise and fall of Christianity. We know that persecution is a paramount reality in today's world. Open Doors, an excellent ministry that exists to serve persecuted Christians around the world, warns that each month 322 Christians are killed for their faith, 215 churches and Christian properties are destroyed, and 772 forms of violence are committed against Christians (such as beatings, abductions, rapes, arrests, and forced marriages).[11]

To think that America is immune is naive and the precursor to a dangerous apathy. As pastor and author John MacArthur has noted, "Religious liberty isn't promised to Christians. . . . Persecution is."[12] My friend Brett O'Donnell, who works for a variety of national and state political candidates, has his finger on the pulse of the culture as well as anyone I know. During a conversation at a recent dinner, he said, "Daniel, your grandchildren will be the first generation to grow up in a society where being a Christian and being an American citizen is no longer compatible."

To "sift" means "to separate by or as if by a sieve; to examine or question closely; to isolate that which is most important or useful."[13] I believe a sifting is coming. This is a reality that will separate true Gospel ministry from empty, socially acceptable

A sifting is coming that will separate true Gospel ministry from socially acceptable Christian religion.

Christian religion. A result could very well be the shedding of all things superficial and peripheral. This may well mark the return to very basic, Spirit-dependent, prayer-energized, and Gospel-propelled ministry, irrespective of programs, budgets, and facilities.

The suspicion and hostility within the present culture is growing like a suffocating kudzu vine engulfing a grove of Georgia trees. As I write, the nation is watching Christians being fined and even jailed for not complying with the mainstream establishment of gay marriage. Believers holding a biblical view of marriage are being labeled as "homophobic" by the highest political leaders in the land. The entertainment industry is celebrating all forms of immorality and debauchery in award-winning movies and songs. People who do not embrace this new day are now postured as the misfits and antebellum weirdos.

Already, Christian schools are being threatened to comply with the normalization of unbiblical lifestyles in the official documents of the institution or risk losing accreditation and government-sponsored loans for their students.[14] Many leaders are convinced that the day is approaching quickly when tax-deductible giving to Gospel-rooted churches and Christian organizations will be taken away. When the government decides to tax churches for their land and buildings, the large facility-dependent, program-driven mega-ministries will likely falter.

In Their Own Words

Watch H. B. London ("America's Pastor to Pastors") describe the unique challenges of "Pastoring in the 21st Century" at http://www.64 fellowship.com/resources/oldpaths/02/

A HOPEFUL PREPARATION

The best preparation for the future sifting is a return to the realities that gave early church leaders a transcendent faith and extraordinary impact. I have personally witnessed this kind of devotion on multiple occasions within the house churches of China where the greatest current-day revival and advancement of Christianity have occurred under the oppression of a communist government. With no facilities, no social media, no large programs, Christianity has flourished. Ministry in China is led by humble Christian leaders and the people are doing one-another ministry reminiscent of the New Testament. Old paths. New power.

Back here at home, with all the training, technology, wealth, talent, and unprecedented opportunities we now have at our disposal, we are losing ground. So the sifting has begun. In all likelihood, it will become more focused and intense. Fortunately, the old paths of leader-

Our real problem is not a pervading darkness but a failing light. Light always dispels darkness.

ship seen in the book of Acts are still able to provide new power to face the challenges of ministry in a postChristian culture—even in North America.

It is time to experience a truly transforming ministry approach. As Os Guinness has written:

> Let there be no wavering in our answer. Such is the truth and power of the Gospel that the church can be revived, reformed and restored to be a renewing power in the world again. There is no question that the good news of Jesus has effected powerful personal and cultural change in the past. There is no question too that it is still doing so in many parts of the world today. By God's grace it will do so again even here in the heart of the advanced modern world where the Christian church is presently in sorry disarray.[15]

Our real problem is not the pervasiveness of the darkness but a failure of the light. Light always dispels darkness. The glorious light of the resurrection life of Jesus Christ is still sufficient and available to those who reject self-reliance and return to His plan for biblical leadership. This return can reignite the radiance of the Gospel in transforming power.

In America our big challenge is that in many cases we do not recognize our need to be awakened. We may be like the church of Sardis in Revelation 3:1–6—living in the false reality of a former glory, still believing we are full of life, effective, and fruitful—when we are really comatose. Could it be that our reputation has far exceeded our spiritual reality? Recall Christ's words of warning to His followers in Sardis:

> "I know your works. You have the reputation of being alive, but you are dead. Wake up, and strengthen what remains and is about to die, for I have not found your works complete in the sight of my God. Remember, then, what you received and heard. Keep it, and repent. If you will not wake up, I will come like a thief, and you will not know at what hour I will come against you." (Rev. 3:1–3)

You may be in the leadership of a church that is in clear need of a reawakening to the sufficiency of the Spirit and authority of Christ. All the indicators are pointing downward and the need is obvious. On the other hand, you may be in a ministry that seems to be hitting on all cylinders. Attendance is strong, programs are flourishing, and the momentum is upward. Yet the question must still be asked about whether our works "are complete in the sight of God." We must honestly assess the level of life transformation, extraordinary prayer, Spirit-empowered preaching, authentic evangelistic living, and fruitful disciplemaking. Like the believers at Sardis, we need the grace to wake up, strengthen what remains, remember all that we have heard and received, and embrace these things in a vital awakening.

Let us affirm with all our energies that we need a personal, congregational, and national revival; one that might spark a sifting, leading to a full Great Awakening. Or, perhaps we need a sifting, prompting a revival, leading to a Great Awakening. In either case, we need a fresh and powerful work of the Holy Spirit. Short of revival we are simply running laps on the Titanic. As we enjoy the titillation of our self-contained evangelical culture, the ship is headed for disaster.

Here's the good news: Christ offers a new experience of His power to face these challenges to all who will return to the old paths of the New Testament pattern. As G. K. Chesterton has observed about church history, "At least five times the Faith has to all appearances gone to the dogs. In each of these five cases, it was the dog that died."[16] Let us believe that the "dog" of our current drift will die in the fire and heat of the new power Christ offers the church.

Lord of the years, sovereign over time and history, speak to us in power by your word and Spirit, and so break into the shortsightedness and error of our understanding. Help us to distinguish the true from the false, the enduring from the passing, and the costly from the cheap. . . . Give to us such a clear understanding of the times in which we live that we may serve your purposes in our generation and be more truly your people in our world today . . . In the name of Jesus, Amen.[1]

OS GUINNESS

Jesus has not called us to figure it out but to follow Him.

ANONYMOUS

2

An Urgent "Leadership" Renovation

Celebrate Recovery is a program that has franchised its way into thousands of churches across the evangelical landscape, providing a practical path of freedom for those captured by addictions of various shades. I've never attended a CR meeting, but if one existed just for pastors I would have gone, and I know what it would have been titled: "Leadershipaholics Anonymous."

You see, for many years I was a fanatical leadershipaholic. Enamored by the influence, insight, and ingenuity of high-profile impact players, I devoured books on leadership like a contestant in Nathan's International Hot Dog Eating Contest on a warm July day in New York City. Like the obtrusive bill on a pelican, the section on leadership in my personal library was pronounced and filled with the latest and greatest catch of the moment, lying just below the surface of my quest for maximum personal potential. I waited with palpable eagerness for the next leadership conference so I could hear the sage insights of church, business, and even political leaders as they gave me the next golden ticket for pastoral success.

To embrace the old paths of biblical influence we must identify new paths and evaluate their nature. To do so requires an honest assessment of our current obsession with a good thing that has become "the" thing—and perhaps kept us from the essential thing.

Some days I wonder if present-day evangelicalism can even function apart from the word *leadership*. The concept has almost become an idol in pastoral ministry. Certainly, the glut of books, conferences, seminars, blogs, podcasts, and simulcasts about leadership far outweighs gatherings to understand or experience the person and power of the Holy Spirit. We are bored with the old-fashioned notion of Spirit-empowered, Spirit-guided, and Spirit-produced impact. These doctrines seem too familiar, maybe elementary, and rather passé, best valued by the out-of-step, old-school guys. We assume, and functionally dismiss, many truths about the Holy Spirit, but we are definitely skilled at articulating endless discoveries about how to influence, manage, and maximize our strengths. Announce a new leadership convention or an innovative management book and we gather like mosquitos on a summer sunbather on the shore of a Minnesota lake.

The other day I downloaded five leadership podcasts produced by a popular pastor, not because I have an appetite for his ideas, but just to see what is on the menu that sustains so many of my ministry colleagues. Five podcasts later, I knew all about savvy management principles. I repeatedly heard all the reasons why I should try to imitate other shrewd leaders for my important decision-making. I gained some splendid insights about human behavior in staff settings. I even felt that if I wanted to be cutting edge, I needed to download five more presentations. Of course there was some value in these things and we can learn from anyone who imparts fundamentally sound ideas.

Not to be a crank about it, but I did notice that not one mention of Christ, the Holy Spirit, prayer, humility, or any of the salient themes in Jesus' earthly ministry made the cut. Leadership seems to be the new fascination of pastoral ministry. We are consuming this stuff like zombies looking for warm flesh on *The Walking Dead.* Like the morbid spooks on the popular end-of-the-world show, we hear a noise that sounds like some leadership grub and we stagger off en masse to find a tasty morsel. But where is it getting us, and is it providing the essential nutrients for transforming a lost world?

In Their Own Words

Watch Pastor Keeney Dickenson (First Baptist Church, Crockett, TX) speak openly about "Prayerless Leadership," his "bookaholic" mentality, and the role of pastors in revival at http://www.64fellowship .com/oldpaths/03/

WHAT IS LEADERSHIP?

It's been said many times that when a truth becomes "the" truth, it results in untruth. I have concluded we have overreached, overestimated, and oversold the whole leadership theme. Renowned business writers Warren Bennis and Burt Nanus reported in their research that they have discovered more than 850 different definitions of leadership.[2] It seems we have examined the topic to such an extreme that we do not even know what it is anymore.

Of course, leadership is a useful enabling in the hands of God. It is a gift God bestows for the benefit of the church. A leadership definition I like is offered by Kenneth O. Gangel, "The exercise of one's spiritual gifts under the call of God to serve a certain group of people in achieving the goals God has given them toward the end of glorifying Christ."[3]

A proper definition of leadership is vital. Why? Because a biblical definition of church leadership is fundamental to a work of revival. We must evaluate the real essence of our calling and identify the shiny objects that lure us away from that duty. I am convinced that the great impediment to a new experience of spiritual power in the church may not be spectacular sins but subtle self-reliance.

Biblically, "leadership" is mentioned as a spiritual gift (Rom. 12:8) and, interestingly, further toward the bottom of the list. The concept appears in 1 Corinthians 12:28, again toward the end of the sequence. The original meaning in the Greek is to "stand before." The word was used to describe an individual who steered a ship.

Like all gifts, God sovereignly bestows leadership for humble service to the body of Christ. I don't want to belittle this significant gift, since I have been given that gift for my own ministry assignments, but simply desire to point out that we have blown it way out of biblical proportion. Perhaps of greater concern is that we have taken leadership, a supernatural gift, and turned it into a finely honed strategy. By doing so we have diminished the supernatural character of leadership and made it just another tool in the drawer of ecclesiastical performance.

We have taken leadership, a supernatural gift, and turned it into a finely honed strategy.

Further, it seems our pursuit is contrary to what Jesus actually taught. Here were our Lord's exact words and the context that prompted His incredible wisdom:

> Then the mother of the sons of Zebedee came up to him with her sons, and kneeling before him she asked him for something. And he said to her, "What do you want?" She said to him, "Say that these two sons of mine are to sit, one at your right hand and one at your left, in your kingdom." Jesus answered, "You do not know what you are asking. Are you able to drink the cup that I am to drink?" They said to him, "We are able." He said to them, "You will drink my cup, but to sit at my right hand and at my left is not mine to grant, but it is for those for whom it has been prepared

by my Father." And when the ten heard it, they were indignant at the two brothers. But Jesus called them to him and said, "You know that the rulers of the Gentiles lord it over them, and their great ones exercise authority over them. It shall not be so among you. But whoever would be great among you must be your servant, and whoever would be first among you must be your slave, even as the Son of Man came not to be served but to serve, and to give his life as a ransom for many." (Matt. 20:20–28)

This aspiring mother wanted significance for her sons. Jesus responded by elevating sacrifice and selfless abandon. Jesus exposed the world's view of leadership as an exercise of ambition in pursuit of position. Then He affirmed, "It shall not be so among you." His way of providing guidance and having influence was to serve as a slave. A slave is one owned by another, having no rights. Those who aspire to exercise a gift of guidance for the church must embrace complete obedience to their owner, Jesus Christ. And He is our example as One who came "not to be served but to serve and to give His life a ransom for many."

Our modern pursuit of "leadership" is often interlaced with aspirations for prominence, based on a desire to be someone of significance. Our paradigms are rife with competition, self-promotion, and notoriety. And what is behind it all?

I remember sitting with Henry Blackaby enjoying lunch as we took a break from speaking at a conference in North Carolina. As we interacted about the current state of church ministry, he offered a perspective I will never forget. With erudite wisdom he said, "I am convinced that there are more men in pastoral ministry today motivated by insecurity rather than calling." That resonated. Maybe it was just me, but in the early years of ministry I learned the thorny lesson that my carefully veiled insecurities, ambitions, and enthrallment with "bigger and better" were not exactly harmonious with God's Word or God's glory.

I wish I could say that in my decades of pastoral ministry, I exercised the gift biblically, meekly, unselfishly. But that was not the goal of my leadershipaholic bent. I never want to go back to that old pursuit again, now that I have discovered something so much better and more compelling.

WHAT'S THE BIG DEAL?

You may ask why I am picking on our modern concepts of leadership. Three reasons:

First, pastors have limited time, energy, and attention. We must allocate our treasured personal resources in a manner that is biblical and that can facilitate a genuine, supernatural work of the Holy Spirit. Chasing after lesser things produces diluted, shallow, even man-centered ministry.

Second, I have concluded that the devil does not care what we replace the centrality and sufficiency of the Holy Spirit with—as long as we replace Him with something. In my view, "leadership" has become the prevalent substitute of choice. And, yes, it "works." Leadership accomplishes a lot in business and even in the cults. But a productive and subtle self-reliance diminishes the person and power of the Holy Spirit in the work of Christ.

Third, because artificial models produce superficial results. We are imitating one another into spiritual oblivion. Yet, the prototype of New Testament leadership is still sufficient and essential. When we seek to imitate the "success" of other talented superstars, we fall short and the fruit is plastic rather than life-giving.

AN ALTERNATIVE BIBLICAL APPROACH

For many years, I read through the Bible every year, utilizing many versions and plans, for my personal growth. But as my enthrallment with the leadership glitter began to tarnish I determined to discover what the Bible explicitly taught about those to whom God had entrusted significant spiritual influence.

In reading the Scriptures it became evident that the primary common denominator of those individuals used by God was centered in the simple phrase, "the Lord was with him." Certainly, every biblical leader had a mix of natural attributes and developed skills, but these are seldom mentioned. Rather, the primary secret to their excellence was a genuine and manifest sense of the presence and power of God. This factor was an essential issue of the heart and is best understood and sustained in current-day ministry by a fullness of the Holy Spirit via a humble, enduring, and prayerful walk with God.

In the Old Testament, this phrase was descriptive of Abraham, Isaac, Jacob, Joseph, Moses, Joshua, and David, as well as some of the significant judges, kings, and prophets. In the New Testament it was said of John the Baptist, Mary, and the disciples. [4] Of course, in His final commission Jesus did not reassure us by saying "And, behold, you will guide the church by becoming skillful leaders and dynamic visionaries, even to the end of the age." Rather, His words were clear, precise, and compelling. "Behold, *I am with you* always, to the end of the age" (Matt. 28:20, emphasis added).

When we compare Matthew's account with our Lord's famous last words in Luke and Acts (Luke 24:49; Acts 1:8), it is clear that Jesus is referring to an imparting. He speaks of a permanent indwelling and supernatural empowering of the Holy Spirit, apart from whom we can do nothing. So our great pursuit should not be pop-culture notions of leadership. Rather, we should align our passions and priorities to ensure that the fullness and fruit of the Holy Spirit are the compelling flagship and force of our ministry.

Our conventional, modern-day pursuit of leadership, for all of its practical benefits, tends to be about what we can devise for

Christ. The priorities of prayer and the ministry of the Word are clearly about that which Christ wants to initiate then perform through us. This is a lesson the great evangelists have learned. Jim Cymbala saw the truth the one time he met Billy Graham at his Montreat, North Carolina, home. Graham's grandson Will invited Cymbala, who had spoken the previous night at The Cove (a beautiful retreat center operated by the Billy Graham Evangelistic Association) to come visit the evangelist. Cymbala's message had focused on the Christian's primary calling to "be with Jesus" in deep fellowship and humble dependence—and then to serve as the overflow of that intimacy.

After introductions and warm conversation, Will (who directs The Cove's operations) described his excitement at the message on the priority of intimacy and prayer as key to preaching. As Will spoke, Dr. Graham raised his hand to stop him. Then Graham said, "That's for me. That message is just for me. That is what I really need . . . to be with Him."

OF PARAMOUNT RELEVANCE: BEING HUMBLE

The following passages highlight the apostle Paul's framework for spiritual influence. Many may be familiar to you, but I trust you will read them with fresh eyes. Paul underscores something other than our familiar emphasis on the dynamics of refined human influence. Paul's old paths of spiritual impact are demonstrated throughout his letters, but a few excerpts can bring the point home. We begin with First Corinthians 2:

> And when I came to you, brethren, I did not come with superiority of speech or of wisdom, proclaiming to you the testimony of God. For I determined to know nothing among you except Jesus Christ, and Him crucified. I was with you in weakness and

in fear and in much trembling, and my message and my preaching were not in persuasive words of wisdom, but in demonstration of the Spirit and of power, so that your faith would not rest on the wisdom of men, but on the power of God. (vv.1–5 NASB)

By today's standards, Paul was unimpressive and was clearly disinterested in any sophisticated and high-powered principles of "kingdom impact." His passion was not to attract listeners to his ministry but to be sure they were awed by the power of God. In a subsequent letter to the Corinthian church he amplified:

Not that we are adequate in ourselves to consider anything as coming from ourselves, but our adequacy is from God, who also made us adequate as servants of a new covenant, not of the letter but of the Spirit; for the letter kills, but the Spirit gives life. (2 Cor. 3:5–6 NASB)

Inadequacy is not a popular notion in the featured workshops at our church-growth symposiums. The amazing truths of the life-giving work of the Spirit seem to have fallen off the page on the programs of many of our national conferences. Still, the apostle's words ring relevant: "But we have this treasure in earthen vessels, so that the surpassing greatness of the power will be of God and not from ourselves" (2 Cor. 4:7 NASB).

We elevate great leaders, famous speakers, extraordinary talent, enormous churches, remarkable strategies, impressive formulas, and stirring human insight. Yet the real treasure is paramount and available in hearts of inadequate servants who seek the face of God as the core of what it means to oversee the work of Christ. That is what Paul did, and he listened to God's reply: "He said to me, 'My grace is sufficient for you, for power is perfected in weakness.' Most gladly, therefore, I will rather boast about my weaknesses, so that the power of Christ may dwell in me"(2 Cor. 12:9 NASB).

The more we value and embrace weakness, the more delight

Christ finds in making His power known in and through us. This is not the theme of most leadership books or conferences I have encountered. Yet Paul reminds us of the ultimate challenge every spiritual leader faces:

> For we do not wrestle against flesh and blood, but against the rulers, against the authorities, against the cosmic powers over this present darkness, against the spiritual forces of evil in the heavenly places . . . praying at all times in the Spirit, with all prayer and supplication. To that end keep alert with all perseverance, making supplication for all the saints. (Eph. 6:12, 18)

Paul reminds us that our primary task is to triumph in the face of an unseen but paramount spiritual battle. Because the conflict is fundamentally spiritual, the only way we win is through spiritual means. Paul emphasizes the imperative of pervasive, all-encompassing prayer—that the Lord may be with us.

HIS DELIGHT: OUR HOPE IN HIM

God's delight, prompting the blessing of His unmistakable presence, remains the same today regardless of our multitude of other appealing options:

> Thus says the Lord: "Let not the wise man boast in his wisdom, let not the mighty man boast in his might, let not the rich man boast in his riches, but let him who boasts boast in this, that he understands and knows me, that I am the Lord who practices steadfast love, justice, and righteousness in the earth. For in these things I delight, declares the Lord." (Jer. 9:23–24)

God's pleasure abounds toward the inadequate servant who rejects all self-boasting. His delight is not in an adroit ministry guru who is ready to profit from those in need of a new, productive strategy, but in those who hope in Him. "His delight is not in the strength of the horse, nor his pleasure in the legs of a man, but the Lord takes pleasure in those who fear him, in those who hope in his steadfast love" (Ps. 147:10–11).

As it has always been throughout biblical history, God looks upon the heart. His pleasure is upon the soul that is fixed on Him; the heart that hopes in the power of the relationship, not the production of human enterprise.

> The king is not saved by his great army; a warrior is not delivered by his great strength. The war horse is a false hope for salvation, and by its great might it cannot rescue. Behold, the eye of the Lord is on those who fear him, on those who hope in his steadfast love. (Ps. 33:16–18)

Relying on our own resources is a misleading road to mediocrity, even disaster. God's attention and blessing rest on the life that has a high view of His power and an assurance of unfailing love.

LANGUISHING IN LAODICEA

One of my favorite childhood cartoon series was *The Flintstones*. Fred, Wilma, Betty, and Barney, along with the kids and the critters, captured my imagination with their ever-exciting lives in Bedrock. I loved the closing seconds at the end of each show. Fred puts the family cat out for night. He then puts the milk bottles on the front porch, not noticing that the cat has raced inside and proceeds to lock Fred outside. The scene closes with Fred banging on the outside of the door frantically, yelling "Wilma! Wilma!" As a kid, I always found it so funny to see Fred locked out of his own house, unable get in.

The glorified Christ described a comparable scene in Revelation 3 as He addressed the church in Laodicea regarding their spiritual condition. That church's reality was jarring and certainly was not so funny. The church members thought of themselves as "rich, . . . and [in need of] nothing" (v. 17). The Lord saw it differently. He told them they were poor, wretched, miserable, naked, blind, and in need of a spiritual awakening. Their problem: Jesus was on the outside looking in as they reveled in their self-sufficiency. He stood at the door of the congregation knocking, eager for reentry. Appealing to them to repent and recognize their prosperous but dangerous spiritual indifference, He gently invites them to open the door.

I often wonder how Jesus got on the outside of this church. Some say the church was unregenerate, but I do not think He would call it a "church" of people He loved if this was the case. Rather, I think their self-sufficiency, pride, and human activity shoved His presence from the center of attention to the back porch.

The frightening observation about the Laodiceans was the subtle reality that self-sufficiency had blinded their eyes to the degree that they denied their true condition. They failed to even realize that Jesus was no longer fully present among them.

I have concluded that our obsession with leadership is rooted in a culture of achievement. The Scriptures are clear that New Testament ministry is not about what we can achieve but rather how willing we are to receive. But if we are to receive, we must open the door, surrender our hearts, and return to the paths that invite His presence and power. As Paul asked the competitive and carnal Corinthians: "What do you have that you did not receive? If then you received it, why do you boast as if you did not receive it?" (1 Cor. 4:7). May we never "act out" as spiritual achievers.

Rather, may the Lord be with us.

In Their Own Words

Watch Trey Kent (pastor, Northwest Fellowship, Austin, TX) describe his "Influence in Ministry as the Overflow of Intimacy" at http://www.64fellowship.com/oldpaths/04/

Whether Old or New Testament we see that God wants us to know His received life and with that His received works and received ministry. . . . Ministry must be received by faith, never achieved by flesh.[1]

RICK SHEPHERD

Our activity for God can only flow from a life with God. We cannot give what we do not possess. Doing for God in a way that is proportionate to our being with God is the only pathway to a pure heart and seeing God.[2]

PASTOR PETER SCAZZERO

3

Vision: Received or Achieved?

I 've always had a fascination with flying. My dad was a bomber pilot in the Air Force. I was recruited by the Air Force Academy my senior year in high school but chose instead to go to a small Christian college on scholarship to prepare for pastoral ministry. (Honestly, I've often wondered about that decision, as I never did learn to fly.) When I was a young pastor, living near the Seattle–Tacoma Airport, I would take my "portable" Zenith computer, the dimension of a medium-sized suitcase, and find a perch in the American Airlines Admiral's Club overseeing the runway. As I "studied" for my sermon, I would watch take-offs and landings, dreaming of the adventure represented in each flight.

The experience of soaring 35,000 feet above the earth, heading to a new destination to engage a fresh adventure, is in my blood. Beyond this, looking down on the world from the heavens offers a rare perspective. Soaring above the clouds, the troubles and frenetic pace of humanity seem insignificant. I can escape the daily concerns and capture moments of reflection as I think about my journey and some of the transcendent realities of life.

Several years ago I was flying from California to Pennsylvania to speak at a pastors' conference. As was often the case, I was reading another book on leadership. The author had some great thoughts, but this was the time when I was second-guessing my obsession with the whole leadership pursuit. As I closed the book, spiritual conviction overwhelmed my soul. Without any warning, I began to weep as I surveyed the clouds below. (Thankfully, I had the entire row to myself, which minimized the embarrassment.) I prayed:

"Lord, all my life I have been striving to be a powerboat for Christ. The hull of my type-A personality is cutting through the waters of ministry. I've had my hand on the throttle of effective leadership principles. I've filled my tank with the high-octane insights of a seminary education. I seemed to be making an impression with my visionary style. But . . . Forgive me. From this day forward, would You teach me what it means to be a simple sailboat?"

Of course, my mind was surging with the reality that a simple sailboat does not bring glory to itself but to the power of an unseen force propelling it along. It is dead in the water unless the wind blows. I knew the course might be a little unpredictable because of the nature of the "wind," but I was tired of trying hard to be a high-impact leader. I knew in the depth of my soul that God was revealing to me a better and more fruitful way.

OLD-PATH RECEPTION

Returning to the example of the apostles in Acts 6:1–7, we see leaders who understood what it meant to be sailboats rather than powerboats. Their persona had been sized up by their persecutors in an earlier chapter. As these unexceptional fishermen were under interrogation, the text states, "Now when they saw the boldness of Peter and John, and perceived that they were uneducated, common men, they were astonished. And they recognized that they had been with Jesus" (Acts 4:13). Their power did not come by achieving ministry through refined skills and impressive feats of leadership. They were sailboats into whom, and through whom, the wind of the presence of Jesus moved in irrefutable fashion.

This mindset framed their response to the crisis that hit them in Acts 6:1, when the program to feed widows unraveled. I suppose they had enough collective smarts to evaluate the logistics. They could have solved the supply-and-demand snarl, evaluating the food inventories, redesigning the delivery schedule, and achieving some heroic solutions that would increase their likability among the masses that had joined the First Church of Jerusalem. But for them, the ministry was not something to achieve. They had confidence in finding other respected and spiritual men who could reorganize and reinvigorate the meal services.

They were resolute to receive ministry, from Christ, by His Spirit, in the environment of "prayer and the ministry of the word." What He imparted to them, to the church, and through them to the community, was truly transformational and undeniably divine. This seems so counterintuitive for us in today's "get 'r done" culture.

In writing about this Acts 6 moment, John Piper notes, "The effort to meet needs is, ironically, often the enemy of prayer."[3] Trying to achieve can be the blockage to all God wants us to receive. Piper goes on to describe the apostles' response to this real need among the widows:

> But the apostles would not yield to the temptation. This must mean that prayer demands a large part of their interrupted time. If they had thought of prayer as something you do while washing dishes or cooking (or driving a car between hospitals), they would not have seen table-serving as a threat to prayer. Prayer was a time-consuming labor during which other duties had to be set aside.[4]

Tempted to personally achieve a solution for the sake of the widows, their alternative resolve was clear. "We will *devote* ourselves to prayer and to the ministry of the word" (Acts 6:4, emphasis added). The word translated "devote ourselves" (*proskartereo*) represents an inflexible commitment to preserve significant time for prayer and the Word. The meaning is to "persist at" something or to "remain with" something. As Piper explains, "The idea is to be strong and persistent and unwavering in one's assignment."[5]

Martin Luther once responded to his barber who had inquired about his commitment to prayer. In the forty-page response, Luther included these resolute ideas:

> Anything that is to be well-done ought to occupy the whole man with all his faculties and members. As the saying goes: he who thinks of many things thinks of nothing and accomplishes no good. How much more must prayer possess the heart exclusively and completely if it is to be a good prayer![6]

Luther also expressed that prayer "is the hardest work of all . . . a labor above all labors."[7] He noted, "There is no greater work than praying."[8]

In Their Own Words

Watch Bill Elliff (pastor, The Summit Church, Little Rock, AR) speak candidly about "The Secret of Real Impact" at http://www.64 fellowship.com/oldpaths/05/

A COLLECTIVE AND CONSISTENT UNDERSTANDING

Notably the Acts 6:4 commitment—and conviction—does not refer to the apostles' personal prayer lives, although we could assume this. Rather, it refers to their collective focus as a team of leaders, and among the people. We see the culture of the leadership team, which overflowed into the life of the church.

A dominant factor that shaped this mindset was the example

of Christ, who spent forty days "receiving" from the Father before "achieving" His mission on earth (Matt. 4:1–11). As Jesus later chose His core team, after praying all night long, the account says, "And he appointed twelve (whom he also named apostles) so that they might be with him and he might send them out to preach" (Mark 3:14). Their work proceeded from their reception of Christ's life and teaching. Throughout His mission, prayer preceded and succeeded all of His work.[9] The apostles witnessed and experienced this with Jesus.

That is why the Acts 6 moment is not the exception but the rule. We should remind ourselves that this is the same resolve that heralded the day of Pentecost as they waited to receive ministry through the Holy Spirit's arrival and empowerment (Luke 24:49; Acts 1:8). They stayed in that receiving position consistently as they embedded patterns of discipleship in the early believers (Acts 2:42). When they encountered persecution they did not try to design a strategy to ensure their equal rights but, through prayer, looked to God to receive a refill of courage (Acts 4:23–30). When Peter was in prison, the church did not hire a lawyer but sought the Lord for His deliverance (12:5). The second half of Acts was launched from Antioch as the leaders fasted and ministered to the Lord, then received fresh instructions and a missionary calling from the Holy Spirit (13:1–3). When tortured and jailed, Paul and Silas sang and prayed and received miraculous deliverance and new power for witnessing (16:25).

In his book, *Jesus Continued: Why The Spirit Inside You Is Better than Jesus Beside You,* Pastor J. D. Greear describes the days of unceasing prayer leading up to Pentecost, the power of Peter's preaching, and the results of the Gospel at Pentecost. He notes that they prayed for ten days, preached for ten minutes, and three thousand people were saved. Then he adds, "Today, we shuffle the zeroes around: we pray for ten minutes, preach for ten days . . . and only three people get saved. What a difference the placement of those zeroes can make!"[10]

THE "SUCCESS" OF THE FORMULA

Some years ago I received a call from a pastor of a large church. He asked if he could host me for lunch when I came to speak at a conference in the area. He and a staff of three planned to attend, and they had collectively read my book *Fresh Encounters*. He indicated that he had some questions, so we locked in the date.

During our lunch, he recounted his journey at the church. He had served as senior pastor for more than a decade. The church had grown from a few hundred and was approaching two thousand in weekly attendance, with an impressive array of programs and facilities. He described the remarkable success of recent years and then stopped midsentence, overwhelmed with emotion. Through the tears he made a profound statement: "I don't know if what I have accomplished had anything to do with the Holy Spirit. I have been a prayerless pastor."

Once he regained his composure I asked, "Then how do you explain all that has happened over the last decade?"

"I worked the formulas," he responded very matter-of-factly. "I knew the formulas for growth, land acquisition, relocation in a growing area, children's programming, youth events, attractive worship services, staff development, and high-impact sermons." He continued, "Yet, if I were to stand before Christ today, I don't know if what I have done is gold, silver, and precious stones . . . or just wood, hay, and stubble."

This man was a leader. He had captured and communicated "vision" to his church. The people followed. Yet his profound realization in this moment underscored a truth I think we all know. You can build significant organizations, spiritual or otherwise, on the sheer dynamic of "leadership and vision." Ministry can actually be achieved quite impressively in today's society. But the old paths that lead to new power compel us to embrace ministry as something to be received.

Today this colleague continues in pastoral ministry with a true passion for other leaders. He recently listed among his top prayer requests a desire (1) for godly, Spirit-filled leaders, (2) life-changing encounters with God in worship, and to (3) lead his church in developing a dynamic culture of prayer.

I reiterate: I am convinced that the devil does not care how we replace the Holy Spirit for other options as long as we replace Him with something. The more palatable and popular the replacements, the more readily we seem to accept them. We would never intentionally neglect good nutrition in exchange for cosmetic surgery simply to feel better about ourselves. But "leadership" formulas and "vision" are so natural and acceptable that they are all the more precarious as replacements for the old paths of ministry.

THE "VISION" THING

As I've hinted, another overblown and overused idea in modern ministry is "vision." No doubt the Lord imparts His plans and ways to the hearts of men. But our obsession with the modern notion of "vision" has eclipsed actual biblical teaching and overshadowed other truths that are much more central to Gospel ministry.

In our environment of accomplishment, we feel driven to come up with a vision, a compelling picture of the future that will rally the troops, raise the funds, and grow the numbers. I remember when we would have a "vision" Sunday early in my ministry. This was usually about my need to "motivate" the church for the sake of greater accomplishments. I would research what others were doing, take the best ideas from the conferences I had attended, throw in a few abbreviated prayers, mix it together with a couple of passages taken out of context, and then serve up this recipe for the sake of the lost people we desired to reach. Again, *vision* is a word we have used way out of proportion with what is merited by the Bible.

Pastor Jim Cymbala writes,

> The concept [vision] has been borrowed from corporate business plans (not the Bible) and sold to us as a tool to help churches grow. I believe it has done untold harm. Often the resulting vision clearly contradicts God's purpose for *his* church. . . . Ministers who become CEO's end up producing little, if any spiritual fruit. They're also susceptible to ego trips and early burnout as they attempt to do God's work by relying on their own talent and cleverness.[11]

Business leader and author Warren Bennis has said of vision, "All leaders have the capacity to create compelling vision, one that takes people to a new place, and then to translate the vision into reality."[12] What Bennis says is true, and herein we find a note of caution. Men clearly have the capacity to *create* compelling vision. Business leaders do it. Cults do it. Politicians do it. But the Bible never calls Christian leaders to *create* a compelling vision. Rather, the Bible makes it very clear that no vision is inspired unless it is received from God through an encounter with His holy presence and then results in His glory, not man's.

Henry and Richard Blackaby explain:

> God does not ask his followers to operate by vision. God's people live by revelation. . . . There is a significant difference between revelation and vision. Vision is something people produce; revelation is something people receive. Leaders can dream up a vision, but they cannot discover God's will. God must reveal it. The secular world ignores God's will, so non-believers are left with one alternative, to project their own vision. Christians are

called to a totally different approach. For Christians God alone sets the agenda. . . . The visions that drive spiritual leaders must be derived from God.[13]

REVELATION LEADING TO TRANSFORMATION

Acts 13:1–3 describes the calling of Paul and Barnabas to the mission field. World missions was birthed not because the leaders sat around to create a vision for reaching the world for Christ. Rather, they were fasting and praying to the Lord. They were seeking the Lord with no agenda other than to experience His life and leadership. They did not choose. God did.

This is almost unfathomable for our modern ministry minds. Our culture is marked by phrases like: "Get'er done!" and "Lead, follow, or get out of the way," We've all heard these:

"If you snooze you lose."

"Get in the game."

"Give it all you've got."

Or how about this one: "Don't just sit there—do something"?

The Acts 13 model is a study in the unexpected: "Don't just do something—sit there." The apostles were intense and intentional—not to achieve ministry but rather to attentively receive ministry. Ministry by, from, and for Christ. Ministry that changed the world.

Paul demonstrated the value of hard work in 1 Corinthians 15:10, "But by the grace of God I am what I am, and his grace toward me was not in vain. On the contrary, I worked harder than any of them, though it was not I, but the grace of God that is with me." Clearly, even his hard work was received, not merely achieved. Yet, it seems that so many of us are seeking to produce great effects through leadership, vision, and church growth formulas. We are so close and yet so far from the truth of New Testament ministry.

In 2014, Cymbala wrote, "In the last twenty years there have been more conferences and more books published on church growth than in all the prior history of our country. As new models of how to grow your church have increased in popularity, we have actually witnessed a precipitous decline of Christians in America. The numbers are irrefutable."[14]

In *Emotionally Healthy Spirituality*, Pastor Peter Scazzero shares honestly:

> But work for God that is not nourished by a deep interior life WITH God will eventually be contaminated by other things such as ego, power, needing approval of and from others and buying into the wrong ideas of success and the mistaken belief that we can't fail. . . . When we work for God because of these things, our experience of the Gospel often falls off center. We become "human doings" not "human beings." Our experiential sense of worth and validation gradually shifts from God's unconditional love for us in Christ to our works and performance.[15]

We have more tools for ministry accomplishment than at any time in church history. At the click of a mouse we can access the latest insights, order the finest resources, and purchase high-powered technological aids. We have established buildings and budgets that would blow the mind of pastors from previous generations. And, generally speaking, there is nothing wrong with these tools. But there is a world of difference between simply *using* these tools versus *depending* on these tools. The acid test that reveals the difference is the prayer level of our lives, our leadership teams, and our congregations. Cymbala notes, "Our problem is not with a godless, secular America, but with a church that is increasingly prayerless, compromised, demoralized, and weak. We have drifted away from the Word of God and the power of the Holy Spirit."[16]

THE HOLY SPIRIT IS THE HOW TO

In recent days I have pondered why members of the early church prayed as they did, while we struggle to give even marginal devotion to prayer. I have concluded that the primary difference between the early church and our day is that they actually understood that the Holy Spirit *is* the "how to." Today, we have so many other "how to's" that we view the Holy Spirit as our associate in ministry rather than the source of all ministry. Our problem is that we can "Google" an answer in two seconds. Why should we spend time praying for two hours?

My smartphone is packed with dozens of downloaded apps. It is easy to view the Holy Spirit like an app that I tap when I need some specific assistance. Rather, I need to understand that the Holy Spirit *is* the operating sysem. When I truly embrace this reality, all the other "how to's" (whether leadership, vision, formulas, etc.) become secondary.

Zechariah's words are just as rich with relevance as they were the day they were penned thousands of years ago: "Not by might, nor by power, but by my Spirit, says the Lord of hosts" (Zech. 4:6). The wind of the Spirit is still sufficient, but He cannot propel a sophisticated, self-sufficient power boat. May God help us set our sails and catch the wind as we embrace the old paths to receive new power for a fresh advancement of the Gospel—for the glory of Christ.

In Their Own Words

Watch as Pastor Mike Michener (Westside Fellowship, Elon, NC) opens his heart about "Intimacy vs. Success" (Question 1) at http://www.64fellowship.com/oldpaths/06/

Ministry is its own worst enemy.
It is not destroyed by the big bad wolf
of the world. It destroys itself.[1]

JOHN PIPER

Two elders' wives sat mending their husbands' pants. One of them said to the other, "Poor John, he is so discouraged by his church work. Just the other day, he said that he was considering resigning. It seems like nothing ever goes right for him." The other wife replied, "That's too bad. My husband was saying exactly the opposite. He's been feeling so inspired lately. It seems like he's closer to the Lord than ever."

A heavy silence filled the room as the women continued mending the pants— one the seat and the other the knees.

ANONYMOUS

4

Overcoming Weapons of Mass Distraction

Each day in the United States, nine people are killed and an additional 1,180 people are injured in crashes that are reported to involve a distracted driver.[2] The AAA Foundation for Traffic Safety found that 58 percent of automobile crashes involving teenagers are caused by distracted drivers.[3]

Distraction has also become the great and subtle archenemy of pastoral health and spiritual awakening in today's society. It is not that pastors are fundamentally disinterested in a great spiritual movement in our churches; they are just diverted. As pastors, we are not apathetic about revival; we are just agitated with lesser things.

I often say that the devil does not have to destroy a Christian leader; he only has to distract him. Over time, that distraction will grow like cancer on an internal organ until it drains the effectiveness of a minister through discouragement, dilution, and despondency.

John Piper explains our struggle this way:

> Ministry is its own worst enemy. It is not destroyed by the big bad wolf of the world. It destroys itself. One survey of pastors asked,

"What are the most common obstacles to spiritual growth?" The top three were busyness (83%), lack of discipline (73%) and interruptions (47%). Most of these interruptions and most of our busyness is ministry-related, not "worldly." The great threat to our prayer and our meditation on the Word of God is good ministry activity.[4]

SYMPTOMS OF THE DISTRACTION CANCER

In a *New York Times* article, writer Paul Vitello reported,

> The findings have surfaced with ominous regularity over the last few years, and with little notice: Members of the clergy now suffer from obesity, hypertension and depression at rates higher than most Americans. In the last decade, their use of antidepressants has risen, while their life expectancy has fallen. Many would change jobs if they could.[5]

In 2015, one denomination confirmed those earlier findings. Its research, based on responses from four thousand clergy, found that ministers indicated a higher rate of obesity, high cholesterol, and difficulties from depressive symptoms than the rest of the population. One quarter of the respondents reported significant stress dealing with critical ministry personnel, and 46 percent noted a significant instance of hostility from members upset about not being consulted or questioning their ministry devotion and personal faith.[6]

Dr. R. J. Krejcir of the Francis A. Schaeffer Institute of Church Leadership Development has been actively involved in multiple surveys of thousands of pastors in various settings from 1989 to 2006. Krejcir states, "Over 70% of pastors are so stressed out and burned out that they regularly consider leaving the ministry. Thirty-five to forty percent of pastors do leave the ministry, most after only five years. 100% of pastors we surveyed had a close associate or seminary buddy who had left the ministry because of burnout, conflict in their church, or from a moral failure."[7]

We are a distracted, distressed, discouraged, and even diminished bunch. The war against our focus, fruitfulness, and fulfillment is unrelenting and producing tragic numbers of casualties.

In Their Own Words

Watch as Lance Witt (pastor, Replenish Ministries) unpacks "Keys to Staying Healthy" at http://www.64fellowship.com/oldpaths/07/

SOURCES OF DISTRACTION

What distracts pastors from the ministry? The answer is multifaceted. Not surprisingly, spiritual attacks continue to distract pastors. "The enemy is always launching weapons of mass distraction on my life," declared one pastor friend of mine as he stood in his pulpit with tears running down his cheeks, appealing to his congregation to pray for him. The enemy loves to target us with interferences of any and every kind.

In the early twenty-first century, our increasingly complex information society now tempts many pastors with a much newer distraction: the almost never-ending stimulation from the latest apps, tweets, posts, and text messages. Advertisements appeal to our desire for possessions, and the entertainment media offer the distractions of sitcoms and hit movies that can be viewed anywhere and anytime. In the midst of all of these inducements, who can focus? And we know that email, Facebook, and other social media have made pastors much more accessible to the masses than could have even been imagined twenty years ago. Such distractions can take us away from our family and times with God.

Ironically, distractions can also be the fruit of trying to please people. Pastor Carey Nieuwhof writes,

> Leadership is inherently difficult because it requires a leader to take people where they don't naturally want to go. So you have a choice as a leader. You can focus on leading people, or focus on being liked. When you focus on being liked, you will instinctively try to please the people you're leading. And when you do, you will become confused. Pleasing people is inherently confusing because people don't agree. One person wants it one way. Another wants it another way. And soon, you're bending over backward to make everyone happy, which, of course, means that in the end, you will end up making no one happy, including yourself. It's actually a recipe for misery for everyone.[8]

Of course, we can easily be tempted to find our worth in the opinions of needy people. We will tend to live in desperate pursuit of an elusive equilibrium. Ernest Becker warned, "Groups 'use' the leader sometimes with little regard for him personally, but always with regard to fulfilling their own needs and urges."[9]

So because we are high-value targets in the spiritual battle; because our tech-crazy society throws distractions at us like pieces falling from the sky in a game of Tetris; because we struggle with our sense of worth based on productivity; and because we feel relentless pressure from needy and sometimes demanding people, we must be stewards who focus on the highest and best priorities.

Piper concludes that the routines of ministry are the greatest distractions from our focus on prayer and serving the Master:

> What opposes the pastor's life of prayer more than anything? The ministry. It is not shopping or car repairs or sickness or yard-work that squeezes out prayer into hurried corners of the day. It is budget developments and staff meetings and visitation and

counseling and answering mail and writing reports and reading journals and answering the phone and preparing messages.[10]

In a world of demanding ministry, we must prioritize and at times even say no. One of my elders would often challenge me, "Daniel, 'no' is a Christian word." Another mentor often reminded me that "The power of 'no' is in a stronger 'yes'." In current-day ministry the force and clarity of our "yes" must be louder than ever, like a foghorn piercing the sea of suffocating demands. With the press of countless options, our "no" must be clear and compelling, based on biblical clarity and conviction.

BIBLICAL PINNACLES OF PRIORITY CLARIFICATION

The Acts 6 example has already informed us of three priorities that were held inviolable by the apostles: (1) prayer, (2) the ministry of the Word, and (3) empowering others to guide major ministry efforts. But there is an Old Testament parallel that merits sober consideration.

If I were to ask you about a paramount moment in the Old Testament when a leader was overwhelmed and in need of clarifying key priorities, you would likely think of Moses. The scene in Exodus 18 tells of Jethro, Moses's father-in-law, paying a visit to Moses, accompanied by Moses's wife and two sons. After an evening of sharing stories and rejoicing in the Lord's mighty deeds in, through, and for Moses, Israel's leader is back at work the next day surrounded by long lines of people in need of Moses's advice and leadership in judging between disputes. Seeing this workload, Jethro responds. "What you are doing is not good. You and the people with you will certainly wear yourselves out, for the thing is too heavy for you. You are not able to do it alone. Now obey my voice; I will give you advice, and God be with you!" (vv. 17–19).

Facing overload and burnout, Moses needs some sage advice and a solution to this untenable situation. Jethro's guidance aims to help Moses and the people survive and thrive. Most importantly, Jethro tells Moses that by complying "God will be with you." There it is again. The mark of real spiritual influence. The manifest presence and empowerment of the Almighty.

Now, most of us would at this point conclude that the essence of Jethro's advice was to "delegate." And, yes, that was part of the prescription but only one-third of the message and the last of three admonitions. Here is Jethro's directive:

> You shall represent the people before God and bring their cases to God, and you shall warn them about the statutes and the laws, and make them know the way in which they must walk and what they must do. Moreover, look for able men from all the people, men who fear God, who are trustworthy and hate a bribe, and place such men over the people as chiefs of thousands, of hundreds, of fifties, and of tens. And let them judge the people at all times. Every great matter they shall bring to you, but any small matter they shall decide themselves. So it will be easier for you, and they will bear the burden with you. (Ex. 18:19b–22)

The advice represents the same three priorities in the same order:

1. *Prayer.* "Represent the people before God and bring their cases to God."
2. *Teaching the Word.* "Warn them about the statutes and the laws" that they may walk in them and do them.
3. *Empowering others to serve.* Find qualified men who can help you judge the people.

Did you notice that in both testaments, at a moment of leadership crisis, the same three priorities emerge in the same order? The result of this focus in Acts 6 was a supernatural explosion of the Gospel. The result for Moses is enough to make most of us covet the outcome. Jethro promises, "If you do this, God will direct you, you will be able to endure, and all this people also will go to their place in peace."

Isn't that what every leader needs and desires? It is our deep-seated longing: that the Lord would be with us; that God would direct us; that we

Prayer. The Word. Empowering others to lead. These old paths can bring new power and fresh joy.

will endure and that peace would reign in the hearts of the people we shepherd. Prayer. The Word. Empowering others to lead. These are the old paths that can result in new power, fresh joy, and authentic perseverance.

THE HIGHEST FIVE

While preserving these three core elements, over the years I have clarified *five priorities* ("yeses") in my pastoral ministry of several decades. They represent the old paths of biblical focus and have consistently delivered me from draining distractions. In summary, I sought to *maintain, model, master, multiply, and mobilize* within these clarified decisions.

1. Maintain

My first priority was to maintain an exemplary Christ-honoring life (1 Tim. 3:2–7; 4:12, 16; Acts 20:28; 1 Peter 5:3; 1 Cor. 11:1; Phil. 4:9; Titus 2:7–8). Primary focus must be on one's spiritual, emotional, mental, physical, marital, family, and relational health. Without it, credibility and ministry will fail. It's been said, "Example is your most powerful rhetoric."

2. Model

Second, I resolved to model a commitment to prayer (Mark 1:35; Luke 6:12; 9:28; 11:1; 22:39; Acts 1:14; 6:4; Rom. 15:30; Col. 1:3; 4:2). The prayer level of any ministry never rises any higher than the personal example and passion of the primary leader. We cannot point the way—we must lead the way.

Spurgeon noted, "Sometimes we think we are too busy to pray. That is a great mistake, for praying is a saving of time. . . . If we have no time we must make time, for if God has given us time for secondary duties, He must have given us time for primary ones, and to draw near to Him is a primary duty, and we must let nothing set it on one side." Spurgeon concludes, "Your engagements will run smoothly if you do not forget your engagement with God."[11]

Martin Luther said it this way:

> It is a good thing to let prayer be the first business in the morning and the last in the evening. Guard yourself against such false and deceitful thoughts that keep whispering: Wait a while. In an hour or so I will pray. I must first finish this or that. Thinking such thoughts we get away from prayer into other things that will hold us and involve us till the prayer of the day comes to naught.[12]

When Acts 6:4 describes the apostles as being "devoted" to "prayer and the ministry of the word," the verb is from καρτερὸς, which means *strong, staunch*, and originally, "to persist obstinately in" or to "adhere firmly to."[13]

3. Master

Third, I committed to master the study of God's Word (1 Tim. 4:6, 13–15; 5:17; 2 Tim. 4:1–2; Acts 6:2). When I teach seminarians and speak to young pastors about preaching, I remind them that, over time, the process is more important than the product. Nothing is easier today than to produce a clever sermon, given all of the podcasts, video illustrations, and content-rich websites. Yet, the cultivation and conviction of earnest study is what produces the character of a pastor and infuses his preaching with passion and application. This "conviction to "study to show myself approved" ultimately results in a depth of life that makes the message authentic to the heart of the preacher. The prophet Ezekiel understood this. "Son of man, let all my words sink deep into your own heart first. Listen to them carefully for yourself. Then go to your people . . ." (Ezek. 3:10–11 NLT).

In Their Own Words

Watch this interview with John MacArthur on "Reclaiming Our Pastoral Responsibility" at http://www.64fellowship.com/oldpaths/08/

4. Multiply

Fourth, I resolved to multiply leadership within the church (John 17:6–20; Acts 10:17–38; Eph. 4:11–12; 2 Tim. 2:2). Leaders don't fall off trees. Future generations develop through intentional, biblical, and transparent equipping. We must proactively identify and then shape the hearts and minds of emerging leaders.

For two decades, in nine-month increments, I met with a fresh group of younger men in the church. For many years, we gathered seventy-five minutes each Saturday morning; years later we met on Thursday mornings. My invitation to these men stated, "Leaders make habits out of the things most people don't like to do—starting with getting out of bed." My staff and elders nominated these men, church members already serving in ministry and displaying potential for greater spiritual influence in the church.

My strategy was simple. We would spend a few minutes praying from the Scripture and then enter into spirited discussion and application in connection with the chapters I had assigned for weekly reading. I just selected a handful of books that had most influenced my life.[14] Of course, the reading was helpful, but the free-flowing interaction seemed especially profitable. These men became key influencers in many avenues of ministry in the succeeding years and most went on to disciple other men.

5. Mobilize

Finally, I determined to mobilize the church toward our mission (Matt. 28:18–20; Mark 16:15; John 20:21; Acts 13:1–3; Phil. 3:12–17; 2 Tim. 4:5–8). The goal always should be "to keep the main thing the main thing." Because the Holy Spirit is the "how-to" of ministry, I tried to lead the church to seek His mind, will, and direction for the ministry, involving others with me in prayer, fasting, and full surrender of the fabric and future of the ministry to Him—to reveal God's evangelistic and missionary heart, and for me to be an example and catalyst for His Great Commission.

MOBILIZING THE CHURCH

Notice that while the first four priorities focus on myself and our leaders, the final priority seeks to involve every member. This came about after I moved from the familiar approach I describe as "vision by imitation"—attendance at various conferences, reading books by successful pastors, and seeking to implement what God had apparently blessed in their contexts—to "vision by inspiration."

"Vision by imitation" was often a miserable disappointment, because I was not one of those leaders. To be honest, ambition for achievement drove my strategy.

After studying Acts 13:1–3, where the leaders simply fasted and ministered to the Lord in anticipation of His next step for their ministries, we shifted to "vision by inspiration." We launched a Forty-Day Spiritual Discovery comprised of a churchwide devotional study and prayer guide that we designed for every member of the congregation. We urged everyone to fast in some fashion (solid food, dessert, television, Facebook, shopping, etc.). For me it became my first (and only) forty-day fast from solid food. Of course, we sponsored accelerated prayer opportunities each week. At the end of this united and extraordinary season, the pastors and elders held a prayer retreat to discern what we had "received" during this journey.

With unanimity we came to a conclusion about the ministry direction for the next year. We agreed it would involve a 25 percent annual increase in general fund giving—our present trend was about 10 percent. After much pushback from the finance team, we forged ahead in sharing this plan with the congregation, submitting it to the Lord in our various weekly prayer times. We believed that if we could not trust this process, we might as well throw spaghetti on the wall and just concoct something from the image of smeared tomato sauce.

After an overwhelming vote of approval from the congregation (since they, too, had a vital role in this direction), we began our new budget year on July 1. We did not conduct any stewardship campaign or preach on generosity. We just moved ahead with the things that arose from our forty-day discovery.

We finished that ministry year exactly 25 percent ahead of the previous year, enabling us to fund all the Lord had placed on our hearts to advance the Gospel. Now, this is not some formula for an annual budget increase. Rather, it is an illustration of the priority of leading the people in a credible, prayerful, participatory process of receiving the Lord's mind and will for the church. I've come to believe that He reserves His most fruitful plans for those who maintain the most focused passion—for Him. God is always glad to oblige when we give Him our undivided attention. We continued this process in the years to follow with fruitful results.

PRACTICAL TAKEAWAYS

A return to the old paths requires robust clarity and sustained conviction around clear, biblical priorities. Your list may be different from mine, but be sure the commitments are biblical, distinct, and practical. You must own them—passionately. To be effective, these priorities must relentlessly shape your schedule. Each week the calendar must be organized around these commitments. Otherwise, distractions will tank effectiveness.

Once these priorities are clarified, communicate them to family, board members, staff, and even the congregation. Change agents can be misunderstood, and having a team around you that understands the importance of your priorities will reduce friction and criticism. Staff members will find it easier to define their priorities to complement yours. The church will understand better (although not always) why you cannot comply with their many requests and, hopefully, will see the value you bring to their lives and to the overall ministry when you are focused and ultimately fruitful.

To overcome the enemy's weapons of mass distraction we must make right choices, engage in the best commitments, allocate our time accordingly, and create an environment of understanding. Too much is at stake to be lured away from the old paths. A fresh experience of His power in the everyday trenches of ministry is our greatest and highest need.

In Their Own Words

Watch Jim Leggett (pastor, Grace Fellowship, Katy, TX) offer helpful wisdom on "Rhythms for Spiritual Health" at http://www.64fellowship.com/oldpaths/09/

ON THE PATH TO POWER

Fruit That Lasts
BY FRANCIS CHAN

Periodically I am asked if in my travels I see a difference in the way we pray in America compared to places like Asia and Latin America. My answer is always the same, "Yes, a big difference." The reasons for this contrast may seem subtle, but they are important.

In America, we have other options. There are other ways to fill a room other than through prayer. There are other ways to get people to raise their hand or come forward or cry, other than prayer. There's a way to create the semblance of a movement of God outside of prayer.

Of course, it's not a real movement of God. It is often a manufactured thing. We know how to create excitement. I guarantee you with the right band or right song selection, we can generate something really "cool" whether it was good in God's eyes or not. So we have multiple options. In many other places of the world it's "all or nothing."

And so this is very important because it's ultimately about the true fruit that results when we're abiding. That's the fruit that will last. Sadly, some of us are content with the fake stuff.

Jesus once told Peter, "Satan has asked for you, that he may sift you as wheat." Then Jesus added, "But I have prayed for you" (Luke 22:31–32 NKJV). Jesus prayed. He demonstrated His dependence. Essentially He says, "Peter, do not worry, because I prayed." That's huge. That's a massive inspiration for us.

Paul resolved "to know nothing . . . except Jesus Christ and him crucified" (1 Cor. 2:2). He didn't come with this wise and persuasive speech. He could have, but He chose not to. He said that there was something about that self-reliance and self-exaltation that emptied the cross of its power. Paul didn't want to do that. So it seems all the enhancements that we add to sound intelligent or to make the service work are actually hurting the real cause.

But most of us as preachers don't want to sound dumb. Rather than doing what Paul did, which was to make himself sound less than what he is, I'm always trying to sound more intelligent than I am, or more godly. Paul reminds us that all that stuff diminishes the power. Paul had determined to come to the people in weakness, trembling, and fear. Simple Gospel. In essence, he says, "I'm going to depend on my prayer life—and the prayers of others." Paul asked the Ephesians to pray for him so he could preach boldly as he desired. He had determined to ground himself in reliance on God—and then preach a simple, foolish message. That's a risk for us because either the Spirit comes through or not.

What I often tend to do I (and I'm guessing others do the same) is set things up so that even if the Spirit doesn't do anything, I still don't look like a failure—and I can still feel pretty good. So then if the Spirit does move, then I go from a kind of midpoint of impact to a higher point. But I'm never down here where nothing happens. Why? Because I've got my program set up nice and safely. I've created this cone of protection so that Francis Chan does not look stupid, and this event does not look like a failure. Of course, we try to justify this because it would "discourage the people" if it turned out badly.

But it's not like this in Scripture. The leaders in the Bible always seemed to take the risk. I think of Elijah, who said, "Okay, I'm going to call down the fire from heaven or my head gets chopped off. I don't have a trick ready or some guy with matches over on the side. I'm depending on God showing up. It's going to happen."

It's what we see with Joshua. His determination was, "We're going to march around the city and blow the trumpet, so this better work." It was the same with Paul. He determined, "I'm going to tell you that Christ was crucified. That's going to be enough."

I am learning that the more we trust, and take those steps of faith, the more we really honor the Lord. We have to determine that the Spirit is sufficient and prayer is going to do it. This is all it's ever taken. That is when real thing happens. That's when we really see God move. That's when we see the true, genuine fruit—the fruit that's going to last.

Adapted from an interview conducted by The 6:4 Fellowship (www.64fellowship.com). Used by permission.

AN OLD PATHS PROFILE
PASTOR ROBBIE SYMONS

ROBBIE SYMONS, pastor of Harvest Bible Chapel in Oakville, Ontario, grew up in a religious home, even serving as an altar boy in the Anglican Church. It was not until 1997, after finishing college, that the grace of Christ arrested his soul and he was dramatically converted after a season of deep misery and questioning. A year later, he met his future wife, Gillian, and they were subsequently married. Neither wanted to go into full-time ministry, but God had other plans. Robbie entered seminary full-time and served as an associate pastor for a period of time.

In 2003, God placed a calling and a dream within a small group of people to see a Harvest Bible Chapel come to the Greater Toronto area. Through supernatural circumstances, a core group of people was formed and the momentum was building. It wasn't long before ideas were being articulated, prayer meetings were being scheduled, and plans were underway for the launch of this second Canadian Harvest Bible Chapel.

The church website summarizes the story: "With a Spirit-led resolve to proclaim the Word of God without apology, to passionately worship His only Son, and to believe firmly in the power of prayer, Jesus is building His Church.

Harvest Oakville has experienced the power and grace of the Lord in its growth from a Bible study of 18 people in 2003 to over 3000 worshipers today." In addition, Harvest Oakville has been used by God to plant five churches across Canada during its short history. Robbie states, "My hope for Harvest, in two words, is LIFE CHANGE! The mission God placed within me early on with Him was to *help people realize their full potential in Jesus Christ."*

Robbie's strength since the start of Harvest has been his commitment to boldly proclaim the Word. They are now on the radio daily in the Buffalo/Greater Toronto region. It is because of his commitment to the Word that his preaching ministry is being so blessed. Yet recognizing the essential nature of prayer, Harvest has a dedicated staff to help Robbie raise the bar in prayer.

Today prayer pervades virtually every area of the ministry. Robbie leads the staff in a prayer time every Tuesday morning to start their week together. Every meeting with the elders starts with "prayer and the Word," sometimes taking up half of the total meeting time.

An hour-long pre-service prayer gathering is sponsored on Saturday nights and Sunday mornings. Teams also meet to pray during the services. Robbie leads a monthly church-wide prayer meeting on the third Wednesday of every month where hundreds show up to pray.

In recent months the church has sponsored "Mini-Prayer Summits." These one-day, no-agenda prayer gatherings are scheduled quarterly. The church is also beginning to connect with other pastors and churches, both to participate in united prayer but also to encourage and equip other leaders in effective prayer.

In commenting on his growing conviction about prayer, Robbie often tells his church, "Without prayer, we're dead!" He describes prayer as the easiest and hardest thing they do at Harvest. It is the easiest because of the simplicity of abiding in Christ but the hardest because the flesh fights it and the devil hates it.

As Robbie reflects on his journey and thinks of his pastoral colleagues, he notes, "At its core I honestly believe that many pastors simply do not wholeheartedly believe in prayer. I believe that we have been deceived into thinking that when we can accomplish something we can see, then we are truly productive. Therefore, we get busy 'doing' and lack the faith to understand the true power of fruitfulness is built upon pleading for *God* to do it.

"For many pastors of my generation, or younger, we must align our theology of prayer with our practice of prayer. And for some we need a whole new theology of prayer," he adds. "Simply put, for many young pastors they simply do not live out that 'apart from Christ we can do nothing.' This is when techniques, leadership tactics, and systems start to crowd out simple and passionate pursuit of the Lord. This is what Satan loves to see, because it's so much easier, with way less opposition, to operate in the foolishness of the flesh than in the strength and power and wisdom of the Holy Spirit. If young pastors are not careful and humble, they might actually find themselves pursuing a level of success that God isn't even in. We must, as young pastors, define success by what the Bible actually teaches. This is incredibly important in our day to see leaders raised up with true and Christlike character, Spirit-filled power, and humility-based leadership."

PART 2

PRAYING LEADERS AND THE SUFFICIENCY OF GOD'S SPIRIT

Thirty minutes of Spirit-aided intercessory prayer is more effective than all the new programs and stylistic changes we are constantly tinkering with. Human ingenuity can't be compared to God's power.[1]

JIM CYMBALA

A pastor who feels competent in himself to produce eternal fruit—which is the only kind that matters—knows neither God nor himself. A pastor who does not know the rhythm of desperation and deliverance must have his sights only on what man can achieve.[2]

JOHN PIPER

5

Finding the Conviction to Make a Change

We've heard, read, and preached the stories many times. All four Gospels record a version of Jesus entering the temple courtyards, reacting to the self-serving merchandising, and in three of the accounts declaring, "My house shall be called a house of prayer" (Matt. 21:13; Mark 11:17; Luke 19:46). John's account of this action says, "His disciples remembered that it was written, "'Zeal for your house will consume me'" (John 2:17). The word *zeal* means "fierceness of indignation" or "fervor of spirit."

Commenting on this display of emotion, Stetzer and Rainer write, "Jesus is angry when we use His assembly for anything other than His intended purpose. Specifically He is angry when prayer is replaced by earthly activities. Jesus expects His people to practice praying and encourage others to do the same."[3] They elaborate:

> If your vision is for personal transformation, this will be seen in
> the practice of praying. Strategies, excellence, methods, or even
> commitment cannot substitute for humble dependence on God.
> If our motivation is numerical growth, then we have no real
> reason to pray. Organizational expansion principles will produce
> results relative to your community or "market." Teamwork,
> communication, people skills, and quality control will produce

results. But none of these things will produce substantive results from God in the lives of people. . . . Transformation is [God's] work. We cannot rely on ourselves and see transformation. It is impossible for us to affect life change.[4]

To what degree do today's pastors really desire transformation? In what fashion are pastors feeling a "fierceness of indignation" about a lack of prayer in their churches? What evidence do you see of a resolute practice of prayer in your local church? Honestly, when it comes to understanding and pursuing the old paths of "prayer and the ministry of the word," pastors are all over the map. Like a kaleidoscope of infinite colors, so are pastors in their level of commitment to prayer as a core component of church life.

THE REAL CONVERSATIONS

I remember a candid conversation with a well-known pastor. After a thought-provoking lunch discussion, I asked, "What does prayer look like in your church and staff?" I knew he had authored a book about personal prayer. He responded, "We're not really into that. We have a group of ladies trying to start a prayer meeting but we are going to shut it down."

"Why?" I asked.

He responded, "It will be nothing but a gossip session."

Admittedly, some request-based prayer gatherings do downgrade into gossip. Still, I was stunned by his nonchalant dismissal of the role of united prayer in the life of the church. At best, it seemed the ministry engaged in what I call "zipper prayer"—opening in prayer and closing in prayer.

In another conversation with a key staff leader in a large church, I probed about his seeming aversion to the role of prayer in the ministry. He responded, "I just believe in hard work." Of course, we all believe in hard work. If anything, I am a borderline workaholic. But I prodded further, "And who do you know who is committed to prayer in the church that is not a hard worker?" After struggling to come up with any names, I expressed to him that real prayer is not an excuse for laziness but, in fact, is one of the most arduous engagements I know of in ministry. Prayer is not a replacement for hard work but, in most cases, empowers Christians for even more fruitful work. As the conversation ended, rather tensely, I smelled a smokescreen.

Clearly, some church leaders are content with a "Martha" mindset—serving but not listening to the Master. They do not seem to comprehend the corporate application of Christ's profound words to Mary about the value to pursuing intimacy with Christ as the heart of our work for Christ and the key to eternal reward for our labors (Luke 10:38–42).

On the other hand, I still remember the first time I heard the audio recording of Pastor Jim Cymbala's landmark sermon, "My House Shall Be a House of Prayer."[5] Sitting in my office, I wept as Cymbala spoke with staggering conviction about this nonnegotiable cornerstone of New Testament ministry. He spoke as a pastor who believed and practiced prayer as the "engine" of every element of the church. He spoke of astounding answers to prayer, including the return to faith by his daughter Chrissy. I could not believe

To return to the old paths we must aspire to new experiences of power the Lord intended for New Testament pastors.

an American church was actually demonstrating prayer in such a profound way. Over the years, I've been to the Brooklyn Tabernacle dozens of times, enjoying the prayer meeting, participating in their services, and bringing in more than one thousand leaders to observe and learn.

Most pastors are sandwiched somewhere between the indifference reflected in the above conversations and the off-the-chart passion of Cymbala. Some may even hide behind the "hard work" justification. Regardless, if we are going to return to the old paths we must evaluate our current attitude and aspire toward new experiences of power the Lord intended for New Testament pastors.

In this chapter we will consider seven stages that help evaluate the actual level of engagement in prayer by a pastor. But one quantifiable reality is the allocation of resources. How much of the pastor's time, staff time, or board time is allocated for prayer? What amount of the budget goes toward equipping, organizing, and emphasizing prayer? Do any staff dollars reflect the priority of prayer? How about precious communication resources like space in the bulletin, announcements, video testimonies, and even the web page? I've been astounded to see the sparse visibility given to the priority of prayer on most church websites. By this standard, it would appear that it is really not a primary emphasis. Resources always follow passion.

In Their Own Words

Watch Khanh Huynh (pastor, Vietnamese Baptist Church, Houston, TX) share on "Enduring Pastoral Leadership in Prayer" at http://www.64fellowship.com/oldpaths/10/

SEVEN STAGES FOR
EFFECTIVE PRAYER LEADERSHIP

Clearly some leaders have a passion to see prayer flourish in their lives and churches while others seem complacent. Some pastors give a real priority to prayer while many seem satisfied with lip service. (To understand why we struggle to lead in prayer, see Appendix 1.) In this moment, let's consider the factors that shape a life of influence in prayer.

In recent years, I have enjoyed coaching pastors (via Internet-based live interaction over a period of four months)[6] about their role in shaping a culture of prayer in their churches. One early point of diagnosis in each coaching group involves identifying the key stages that shape a praying leader. If you are a pastor, I hope you will give serious consideration to these stages—or levels of engagement. Some pastors start at a higher level based on strong biblical conviction or lessons learned in the school of hard knocks. Others are on a lower level, struggling to understand or embrace their role of prayer leadership. In any case, all of us can grow and honor Christ as we embrace a greater effectiveness in leading our church to become a house of prayer.

If you are not a pastor, consider the potential of your influence on others—and, of course, pray for your pastor and his onward journey in prayer. Remember, it is almost impossible to be a critic and a loving intercessor at the same time.

1. Complacency

It is hard to comprehend a smug, complacent attitude toward prayer, especially in light of all that was modeled and taught by Christ and everything we read about the role of prayer in the New Testament church. Still, some pastors have utterly dismissed prayer as a significant core of the culture of the leadership team and congregation.

One pastor I know often declared to his church that prayer was "weird," citing a few peculiar experiences he'd encountered with some "prayer warriors." In spite of the clear New Testament teaching, and the countless positive examples of prayer, he dismissed it as an optional sidebar in his personal priorities rather than the core of Christ-honoring ministry.

This complacency is often rooted in such personal issues as previous negative experiences, an introverted personality, or a struggle with personal prayer. I learned early on that we must submit our subjective experiences and biases to the authority of the Scriptures rather than subjecting the teaching of the Scriptures to our personal experiences. Most pastors know this, but a minority still seems to violate this unambiguous principle when it comes to prayer.

2. Cooperation

The vast majority of pastors are at this level of prayer leadership, being at least accommodating toward the value of prayer in the church. Like a husband who dutifully goes shopping with his wife, many leaders willingly cooperate with the "prayer warriors," "the prayer team," "the prayer fanatics," or the ones who seem to have a "gift of prayer." They are encouraged to do "their thing." Typically, this is done to appease the enthusiasts and at least have the option of pointing to a "prayer ministry" announcement in the bulletin. The pastor's personal commitment to lead any of this is negligible.

3. Concern

Often some experience prompts a genuine concern for prayer. Maybe the pastor encounters a personal, family, or ministry difficulty that triggers a greater sense of need for God. Perhaps a book or some other teaching prompts him to give more attention to prayer. The leader may have a concern that stimulates a sermon series on prayer, increased reading about prayer, and even some occasional prayer events in the church. Unfortunately, this concern can wane under the burden of busyness or other high-profile initiatives in the church.

4. Commitment

Over time, concern may grow into a more tangible commitment. At this stage, the leader begins to devote regular portions of his personal time to the prayer efforts. He may feel that he should lead an occasional prayer gathering or insert more prayer into various meetings. He may desire to engage personally with the prayer team to give them encouragement and guidance. The prayer activities and initiatives become more visible as he feels a greater commitment to see prayer become a vital part of the church.

5. Conviction

At some point, commitment must lead to clear, uncompromising conviction. This is the point where everything changes. Essentially, the pastor concludes, "We must become a 'house of prayer' and I must personally lead this pursuit." Typically, a leader will have a gripping persuasion to consistently seek the Lord in his private life. He feels compelled to guide his staff and his church with real certitude in regular and substantive experiences of life-giving prayer. He cannot do otherwise. He recognizes it as essential to his calling and will not relent in his pledge to model becoming a house of prayer by the example of his life.

Pastor Cymbala exemplifies this as well as anyone I know. Springing from an early ministry crisis, Cymbala embraced a strong conviction about prayer that led to uncompromising leadership. He set aside every Tuesday night to lead his people in a focused, extended prayer gathering. More than forty years later, thousands gather each week to seek the Lord because of Cymbala's sustained devotion.

But it doesn't stop there. Most Tuesday mornings Jim leads his staff in a chapel gathering, typically marked by extraordinary prayer. Very often Jim leads special weekend or even weeklong prayer emphases, with enthusiastic attendance by the congregation. In recent months, he has opened the church auditorium for an hour of waiting on the Lord, again on Tuesdays from noon to one o'clock. During a recent visit, I observed Pastor Cymbala simply sitting on the front steps of the church during this hour, silently in prayer, weeping and pouring out his soul to the Lord in sweet surrender. I don't simply admire Jim's example and substantive allocation of time to prayer. I admire the fact that his conviction continues to grow, as an example to his people and an expression of his love and need for the Lord.

During a recent leadership event a few years ago, he said it so clearly and convincingly: "Our people will pay good money to go hear some Christian musician but they won't come to meet with Jesus for free. I take that personally. What am I preaching? Am I leading people to a personality, a church, an event, a denomination? Or am I leading them to Jesus?"[7] A pastor in one of my coaching groups wrote, "True conviction produces passion. Also, if something is a true conviction you do it—you always have time for what you really want to do."

In Their Own Words

Watch revival leader and retired pastor Richard Owen Roberts' observations on "Pastoring a Prayerless Church" at http://www.64 fellowship.com/oldpaths/11/

6. Competency

Most pastors receive no training on how to lead biblical, life-giving prayer experiences. Many of us, including this writer, struggled in our early years to facilitate the kind of prayer times people actually want to attend. Very few pastors received any substantive equipping for this in seminary. As we come to understand the power of the pattern Jesus commanded His followers to embrace (Matt. 6:9–13; Luke 11:2–4), breakthrough occurs.

Soon, leaders learn the dynamics and impact of Scripture-fed, Spirit-led, worship-based prayer. They develop an increased confidence in the sufficiency of the Word of God, the Spirit of God, and the people of God to inspire transforming prayer experiences.

7. Contagion

Admittedly, there is a laboring in prayer that requires perseverance and discipline. But in time, and typically over many years, the Holy Spirit arrests the hearts of a growing number of believers and a palpable movement emerges. Like a contagion, other people catch the fervor of prayer.

Several years into my pastorate in northern California—after teaching on prayer, equipping leaders in prayer, leading multiple three-day prayer summits, meeting a couple mornings every week in prayer—there was a breakthrough. We launched a midweek prayer gathering called "Fresh Encounter," and soon hundreds were coming every week. More prayer gatherings sprang up. Prayer was woven into every worship service. Soon pastors from across the nation were coming to observe and share in what the Lord was doing. And as a result, their congregations began to experience a fresh work of the Spirit in prayer.

When prayer goes viral, people are not excited about "it" (prayer) but are infectious about "Him" (Jesus). Springing from a palpable environment of transforming prayer, church members carry the flame of spiritual passion into every area of church ministry. Prayer pervades ministry team meetings, small groups, age-specific gatherings, the leadership core, and the public services.

WHAT MAKES THE DIFFERENCE? DESPERATION

Since "conviction" is the turning point in propelling a pastor from a casual complacency to catalyzing an atmosphere of spiritual contagion in the church, what makes the difference? I believe it comes down to this: somewhere in the journey, God may introduce a degree of crisis to bring a leader to the point of desperation. Desperation is a catalyst for a praying life. Whether the crisis is a new and unfolding awareness of one's need for God or a calamity that brings brokenness and a disdain for self-sufficiency, God uses it to embed new conviction about the imperative of prayer.

Martyn Lloyd-Jones spoke of our great need for desperation. He noted, "[We] can fight and sweat and pray and write and do all things, but . . . [we are] impotent, and cannot stem the tide. We persist in thinking that we can set the situation right. We start a new society; we write a book, we organize a campaign, and we are convinced that we are going to hold back the tide. But we cannot."[8]

Then he drew this conclusion, "And so we must throw ourselves upon the mercy of God. It is not so much an organized prayer emphasis as it is an act of desperation. And then, and only then, does the power of the Holy Spirit come flooding upon us and into us. And he does in a moment what incremental organization can hardly accomplish in half a century."[9]

> *"We must throw ourselves upon the mercy of God [in] an act of desperation."*
>
> —Martyn Lloyd-Jones

One Ugandan leader, speaking at a conference hosted by my church, announced, "My message to America is desperation or devastation. The choice is yours." He could very well be correct. I have come to believe that desperation can come through crisis or cultivation. As I've said, God often allows the crisis, but we can also embrace a cultivated desperation.

In previous books, I have written extensively on the pattern of what we call the Lord's Prayer.[10] In its fundamental division we find the first part of the prayer is God-ward while the second is man-ward. I like to describe it this way: "He is worthy. I am needy." I have concluded that the more we seek the Lord, with a passion for His worthiness, the more we are gripped with our neediness. Adoration cultivates desperation.

The prophet Isaiah confessed, "Woe is me! For I am lost; for I am a man of unclean lips, and I dwell in the midst of a people of unclean lips" (Isa. 6:5a). This declaration of desperation was not motivated by a circumstantial calamity or some low view of himself. It was prompted by a high view of God. Isaiah gave the reason for his passionate confession: "for my eyes have seen the King, the Lord of hosts!" (v. 5b). A consistent pursuit of God's worthiness produces a deepening understanding of our neediness. Cultivated desperation.

RELENTLESS RHYTHMS

Without fully understanding the impact of it, I committed myself over the years to what I call "relentless rhythms" of worship-based prayer. Early every Sunday morning I met with leaders to pray for an hour of Scripture-fed, Spirit-led, worship-based prayer. On Monday mornings, I prayed an hour with the men in our church. Our staff met several times a week, just to seek the Lord. One night a week, we eventually held a weekly all-church prayer time. I was privileged to lead a couple of three-day prayer summits each year. At a personal level and family level, I sought to maintain parallel consistency. I learned over time that this regular pursuit of His worthiness never let me get too far from a gripping understanding of my neediness. This was not just a resolve to pray. Rather, it was a rhythm of carving out substantive time to seek God's face and then allow Him to arrest my heart to see my great and continual need for Him.

The schedule will differ for every pastor, but the opportunities to cultivate a deeper desperation are countless. The key is to evaluate humbly where we are in the journey toward effective prayer leadership and seek the help of the Lord to grow in our resolve.

DESPERATE FOR PRAYER IN VIRGINIA

Pastor Lon Solomon has led McLean Bible Church in McLean, Virginia, for more than thirty-five years. During that time, the enterprising church has expanded to five campuses throughout the Washington, D.C., metro area. More than fifteen thousand people identify McLean as their home church.

In the summer of 2013, Lon experienced several months of powerful encounters with the Lord. He described this as a personal revival. Returning from his summer break, he called the staff together and sought their forgiveness for his decades of leading as a prayerless pastor. He asked them to join him on their knees that day as they corporately repented of self-reliance and recommitted to a new paradigm of ministry. Lon delivered the same confession and challenge to the entire congregation, not just once, but in two subsequent weekends.

Immediately after that, Lon invited the church to join him in the prayer room thirty minutes before each of the four weekend services at the main campus to call upon the Lord. The other four campuses initiated similar calls to prayer. In the ensuing months, Lon began to visit with other pastors in the area—most of them in smaller churches and many in ethnic congregations. He sought their forgiveness for McLean's non-cooperation and independence, confessing pride and self-sufficiency. This spark ignited an eventual prayer gathering on the steps of the Lincoln Memorial that coalesced almost five thousand people from some four hundred churches throughout the D.C. area. They gathered to pray for the work of the Gospel. A second gathering has been sponsored with even greater attendance and it appears a broad awakening to prayer is igniting in the region.

In recent years, I've been honored to conduct regular staff training and lead prayer experiences as I have done some coaching. As I continue to work with McLean, I am encouraged to see a growing prayer culture and even a sustained weekly staff prayer gathering each Thursday morning. Pastor Solomon demonstrates the power of conviction in the heart of the primary leader. In his late sixties, Lon felt a sense of crisis as he reflected on his earnest desire to finish well and at his spiritual best. He recognized that prayer must be central to this resolve. In a spirit of genuine contrition, he turned to the Lord and received in return a conviction that has changed his entire approach to pastoral ministry. He has often publicly wondered, "I don't understand why it has taken me so long to see this but I am glad it has happened now."

Prayer is one-half of our ministry,
and it gives to the other half
all its power and success. [1]

CHARLES BRIDGES

It is better to let the work go by default
than to let the praying go by neglect.
Whatever affects the intensity of our
praying affects the value of our work. . . .
Nothing is well done without prayer for
the simple reason that it leaves God
out of the account. It is so easy to be
seduced by the good to the neglect of the
best, until both the good and the best
perish. How easy to neglect prayer or
abbreviate our praying simply by the plea
that we have church work on our hands.
Satan has effectively disarmed us when
he can keep us too busy doing things
to stop and pray.[2]

E. M. BOUNDS

6

Leading a Powerful Culture of Prayer

M y friend and fellow pastor Woody Torrence is the smartest guy I know on the subject of cultural change in the local church. His doctoral dissertation concentrated on that very subject. Beyond all his formal education, Woody has discovered that "consistent pressure over time" is the essential factor in transforming the ethos of a congregation.

Having guided Blue Ridge Community Church in Forest, Virginia for over twenty-five years, Pastor Woody has led a significant shift in its culture toward an extraordinary environment of prayer. This has catapulted his church to its present level of profound impact on the community and around the world. Woody was determined to see Blue Ridge become a praying church.

Woody's journey is an inspiring example of how God changes the heart of a leader, radically reshapes the leader's ministry approach, and shows Himself strong through a praying church. For many years, Woody has made his strategic plans for ministry, hoping God would bless his leadership team in what they were trying to accomplish. He describes the process as "trying to breathe life" into all the programs they designed. Woody and his team attended national conferences to see how everyone else was doing ministry and then tried to duplicate those "success stories." Soon it seemed he was trying to "wear someone else's ministry clothes." A year later, he would return to the same leadership conferences only to discover that the "model churches" had already discarded the approach Woody's team was trying to imitate.

A few years ago, God spoke to Woody in his industrious but weary state of being. The sovereign Christ challenged Woody to resign as "God" and let God be God. At that point Woody decided that he and his leaders would seek the Lord first (and as long as necessary) until they had clarity about where God wanted the church to go.

"We had been trying to make Acts 2 happen, but suddenly realized Acts 1 came before Act 2." Woody says, "What tied the 'wait for the Holy Spirit' in Acts 1 to the arrival of the Holy Spirit in Acts 2 was Acts 1:14—prayer!" This turning point was the beginning of what is a genuine culture of prayer that is the essential DNA of Blue Ridge Community Church.

In Their Own Words

Watch Pastor Woody Torrence (Blue Ridge Community Church, Forest, VA) in conversation with Pastor Mike Moran (Interim Pastor Ministries) as they discuss "New Ministry Paradigms Through Prayer" at http://www.64fellowship.com/oldpaths/12/

SEEKING HEARTS

I have enjoyed the privilege of praying with Woody and his leaders. When they pray, they "hit their faces" and stay there until *God* is finished with the prayer time. Three times a day, five days a week, the staff leads in prayer times at the church. Before making any major ministry decisions, they spend significant amounts of prayer together to find the mind of Christ, not just drum up their own ideas. Before they begin new outreach initiatives, they often sponsor 168 hours (one entire week) of continuous churchwide prayer, and they regularly sponsor congregational prayer services.

As the ministry continues to expand, they do not have a fixed agenda about their next steps; they just want the will of God. They always seem to receive it on their knees. The Lord faithfully launches a powerful new chapter of blessing for the sake of people who do not know Jesus in the region, for God's glory.

SEVEN VITAL TRUTHS ABOUT A CULTURE OF PRAYER

A prevailing theme among the majority of pastors associated with The 6:4 Fellowship is the priority of shaping a culture of prayer. There is no formula or cookie-cutter approach, but we have discovered some vital truths that seem to yield consistent fruit.

1. A Culture of Prayer Is Not a Program

A prayer culture is not a prayer "program." In our instant society where we can order drive-thru meals, "Googled" answers, and immediate gratification of all sorts, we are tempted to think that there must be a recipe for fast-paced prayer impact. Accordingly, we tend to think that appointing a prayer team (or part-time staff member) and commencing a few new prayer activities will satisfy the goal. The pastors I work with are learning that launching additional prayer "programs" can tend to attract the same small group of prayer-motivated participants but solicit minimal participation from the majority of the congregation. Prayer is soon viewed as a department of the church or an isolated attraction just for the "prayer warriors." In this scenario, prayer becomes a ministry of the church rather than *the* ministry of the church. There is a difference between a church that prays and a praying church. One has prayer programs. The other develops a prayer culture.

2. A Culture of Prayer Arises at the Epicenter of Leadership

A prayer culture always emanates from the epicenter of church leadership. I often begin the process of developing a prayer culture among churches by asking leaders two standard questions:

1. How much time do the leaders spend together in prayer?
2. What kind of prayer experience is it?

The prayer level of a church never rises any higher than the personal example and passion of the leaders. The quantity and quality of prayer in leadership meetings is the essential indicator of the amount of prayer that will eventually arise among the congregation. It is easy to simply spend time in a perfunctory review of prayer requests before attacking the meeting agenda. More vital is a united enjoyment and pursuit of God Himself.

There is a difference between gathering to "pray about things" versus quality time spent seeking God's face. One approach fixates on telling God what is on our minds. The other seeks to discover what is on His mind, best experienced by worshiping and praying from the Scriptures. When every member of the board, the staff team, and other key leadership teams have become infected with the prayer virus, based on their common conviction and experience, prayer spreads heart-to-heart and life-to-life into every dimension of the congregation.

Speaking to this concern among church leaders, Pastor Donald McDougall writes,

> If they were convinced that their problems are spiritual, they
> would spend more time in prayer meeting than in planning

meetings. . . . If human effort is the means of victory over spiritual forces, then the more believers exert themselves physically, the greater the chance of victory. On the other hand, if the only recourse is to depend fully upon the Lord, then they would spend more time on their faces in His presence, seeking His help. . . . If the church wants to succeed in its God-given mission, its leadership must realize that one of its greatest needs is more prayer meetings, not more planning meetings. If the monthly leadership meetings would give more time to praying than to planning, leaders would soon find a change in attitude, in perspective on ministry, and in results.[3]

McDougall concludes:

The bottom-line objective is for the leadership to face the fact that the church of which they are a part is not their church; it is God's church. And the people they lead are not their flock but very distinctly God's flock. The purpose of their meetings is not to come to a consensus about running the church but to wait upon God to find out how He wishes His church to run.[4]

Leaders often feel pressure from fellow staff or church members to give equal emphasis to other programs (like children, women's ministry, men's ministry, small groups, etc.), just as they do to prayer. Pastor Mark Vroegop explains it well by illustrating that a physical body can live without an arm, a leg, an ear, even an eye. But a body cannot survive without a vital organ like the heart, the liver, or the lungs. He notes that every ministry in the church is vital for optimum body function, but prayer is a vital organ, without which the church is dead. Thus, prayer demands primary attention and effort at every level of the church, especially within the leadership team.[5]

3. A Culture of Prayer Thrives on Experience above Explanation

A prayer culture is fueled by experience, not explanation. A passion to seek the Lord in prayer is more caught than taught. One pastor friend preached on the subject of prayer every weekend for one entire calendar year. He later confessed it yielded minimal results, except to increase the common gap between the congregation's learning and obedience. Head knowledge alone does not create a passion for God in prayer. He later decided to begin to pray, and invite his people to join him. Admittedly, this ignited a much deeper and greater experience of prayer in the hearts of the members.

Starting a regular churchwide prayer meeting is not always the answer. In my journey, I have served as the senior pastor at large, already-overly-programmed churches. I soon learned that finding a time (weekly, monthly, or quarterly) when a significant segment of the church can show up at another gathering, without other competing activities, is quite challenging. Here is a helpful principle: The all-church prayer meeting is seldom the engine of the prayer culture in an already-established church, but it can eventually become the expression of the prayer culture.

When forming a prayer culture, it is best to "build the sidewalks where the footpaths already exist." Many pastors are learning that it is essential to train believers to lead life-giving prayer experiences in every possible environment where people are already connecting. This would include one-on-one conversations, small groups, fellowship classes, ministry meetings, and weekend services. The goal would be that any believer, in any gathering, with any time frame available to them, can lead Scripture-fed, Spirit-led, worship-based prayer experiences.

Early in my ministry, I learned that if I did not intentionally and consistently equip church members to facilitate life-giving prayer, the prayer culture would not grow beyond my ability to show up. So I was relentless in this endeavor, sponsoring five to six training seminars a year. Eventually, this content became a published book.[6] The next chapter will summarize much of what I regularly teach in many venues around the nation, along with a link to a video presentation of the same principles.

In Their Own Words

Watch Pastor Jeff Wells (WoodsEdge Community Church, Spring, TX) offer his wisdom on "Leading Prayer Gatherings" at http://www.64fellowship.com/oldpaths/13/

4. A Culture of Prayer Is Rooted in Community

A prayer culture is rooted in clarity and conviction about community. I am often asked, "Which is more important, private prayer or corporate prayer?" The answer: "Yes." This is like asking, "Which is more important for walking—your right leg or your left leg?" In our Western civilization, marked by "rugged individualism," we have essentially amputated our corporate prayer leg and are pretty lame on the private prayer leg.[7]

For a prayer culture to flourish, leaders and people must have a clear and compelling New Testament mindset about the priority of corporate prayer. Many modern and, frankly, unbiblical attitudes exists in today's church that make this difficult.

I remember the day one of my elders told me, "Daniel, I'm not coming to our prayer times." When I asked for his reasoning, he responded, "First, if I came, I would just be coming to 'be seen by men' and the Bible prohibits that. Second, the Bible says to pray in your 'prayer closet' so I am going to stay home and pray by myself." With his permission, I responded, "Why don't you change your motive and come anyway?" Then I suggested, "We need to expand your prayer closet because it is way too small."

Distinguished professor and pastor Gene Getz writes,

The hallmark of Western civilization has been rugged individualism. Because of our philosophy of life, we are used to the personal pronouns "I" and "my" and "me." We have not been taught to think in terms of "we" and "our" and "us." Consequently, we individualize many references to corporate experience in the New Testament, thus often emphasizing personal prayer. The facts are that more is said in the Book of Acts and the Epistles about corporate prayer, corporate learning of biblical truth, corporate evangelism, and corporate Christian maturity and growth than about the personal aspects of these Christian disciplines. . . . Don't misunderstand. Both are intricately related. But the personal dimensions of Christianity are difficult to maintain and practice consistently unless they grow out of a proper corporate experience on a regular basis.[8]

I teach occasionally at a seminary in Virginia, which includes a significant group of students from South Korea. Frequently, I have heard these students ask their American classmates, "Why do you pray by yourself?" Of course, every morning the prayer chapel on campus is filled with the sound of Korean praise and prayer, while the U.S. students sleep. Not only do the Korean believers have a habit of expressed passion, but they understand what I believe is a truly New Testament sense of vital community. The Western Church, especially in America, needs to practice prayer within the community of believers. Gathering for corporate prayer, empowered by the Spirit, brings vitality to the church and to private lives.

I have heard my Korean students ask their American classmates, "Why do you pray by yourself?"

Charles Spurgeon has called prayer among believers a spiritual heart-check for the local church:

The condition of the church may be very accurately gauged by its prayer meetings. So is the prayer meeting a grace-ometer, and from it we may judge of the amount of divine working among a people. If God be near a church, it must pray. And if He be not there, one of the first tokens of His absence will be slothfulness in prayer.[9]

Of course, the "prayer meeting" may be a churchwide gathering, but it can also be a vital prayer time embedded in a staff gathering, a small group, or a weekend service.

5. A Culture of Prayer Stems from a Powerful, Enduring Motivation

In my prayer journey I've been motivated by many lesser incentives, like guilt, approval before others, and even an ego-driven desire for church growth. Of course, a passion for revival can even trigger more prayers. Yet, in the long run, we must remember that there is a difference between seeking revival from God and seeking God for revival.

Ultimately, a consistent and enduring motive for prayer must be rooted in a reality that never changes. The only enduring motive for prayer is that our never-changing God is worthy to be sought. This amazing reality should motivate our prayers now and will be the only kind of praying we will be engaged in throughout eternity: "Worthy is the Lamb who was slain" (Rev. 5:12; cf. 4:11; 5:9). This Godward, worship-based compulsion remains steady as it is rooted in God's character and the glory of His Son.

6. A Culture of Prayer Prompts Supernatural Mission Advancement

A culture of prayer is always aimed toward the supernatural fulfillment of the Great Commission. Prayer, as seen in the book of Acts, was not primarily therapeutic but transformational, then missional. The apostles are seen seeking the Lord then experiencing fresh passion and power to accomplish His Gospel calling. You never find a long laundry list of personal health needs, financial concerns, or family issues. As Alvin Reid has said, "Prayer is intimacy with God that leads to the fulfillment of His purposes." Acts presents the reality of life, community, and global transformation as the Spirit works through a passionately praying church.

The church I pastored in Minnesota fostered a profound missions effort. Their "faith-promise" pledges each year totaled approximately two million dollars. When I first arrived, they appropriately described themselves as a "missionary church." Soon we adopted the label of a "praying, missionary church." I have learned that if you are a missionary church and not a praying church, you risk the possibility of sending money and missionaries but without the power, blessing, and reward that only comes by the Holy Spirit. If you are a praying church and not a missionary church, you have prayed amiss, allocating the purpose of prayer simply to personal needs rather than Christ's cause. As John Piper has described it, prayer has become a room service intercom rather than a war-time walkie-talkie.[10]

The church as it ought to be: a prayer-birthed, Spirit-empowered, Christ-honoring lifestyle of infectious Gospel witness.

A. W. Tozer challenges our thinking about this balance:

> Our most pressing obligation today is to do all in our power to obtain a revival that will result in a reformed, revitalized, purified church. It is of far greater importance that we have better Christians than that we have more of them. Each generation of Christians is the seed of the next, and degenerate seed is sure to produce a degenerate harvest not a little better than but a little worse than the seed from which it sprang. Thus the direction will be down until vigorous, effective means are taken to improve the seed. . . . To carry on these activities [evangelism,

missions] scripturally the church should be walking in fullness of power, separated, purified and ready at any moment to give up everything, even life itself, for the greater glory of Christ. For a worldly, weak, decadent church to make converts is but to bring forth after her own kind and extend her weakness and decadence a bit further out. . . . So vitally important is spiritual quality that it is hardly too much to suggest that attempts to grow larger might well be suspended until we have become better.[11]

There is no greater joy than seeing a congregation ignited to seek the Lord in Scripture-fed, Spirit-led, worship-based prayer. This contagion spreads to the community as believers become passionate about the person and message of Christ. They cannot help but speak of "what [they] have seen and heard" (Acts 4:20). Mission accomplished. This is church as it ought to be, exhibiting a prayer-birthed, Spirit-empowered, Christ-honoring lifestyle of infectious Gospel witness.

7. Building a Prayer Culture Takes Time

Building a prayer culture takes time. . . and relentless pressure over time. I often say that it is much more a Crock-Pot than a microwave. Visitors to the Tuesday night prayer meeting at the Brooklyn Tabernacle observe the thousands who now come every week to seek the Lord. What they do not see are the years of a small turnout and uninspiring gatherings. What they do see is the fruit of a pastor who would not give up and believed that, with consistent leadership and a learning heart, God would use him to establish a house of prayer for all nations.

I've heard it said that we should not expect a big crowd when God is the only attraction. This was said of prayer meetings. Again, while pastoring in Minnesota, the congregation had funded a 4,200-seat auditorium. Because of this capacity, local promoters rented our facility for regional concerts featuring many well-known

Christian artists. On these Saturday nights, standing-room-only crowds filled the room. Explosive sound, computerized light sequences, smoke, and ecstatic onlookers marked the evening. The following night, we would hold our Sunday evening prayer gathering. It felt like BB's in a tin can. You could have fired cannon in the room and not hit anyone. While hundreds attended, the crowd was negligible compared to the celebrity-artist attraction of the night before.

This is just one of countless examples that the purity and passion of united prayer is often unattractive to modern-day faith culture accustomed to entertainment-oriented events, whether it be on a Sunday, or at a special concert with rock-star "worship artists." It will take time to build a prayer culture.

A WORD ABOUT WARFARE

We do well to remember that the devil hates a praying leader and a praying church. When we begin to pray, we pick a fight with the devil at a whole new level. Yet our calling is to be praying menaces to the enemy.

One subtle arena of attack is in the area of pride. Praying people can become prideful about their praying. Non-participants can become prideful in their resistance. The enemy seeks to divide and conquer every initiative of prayer. (I've written about this in Appendix 2, titled "The Pride Divide.")

This is the reality of building a culture of prayer. I define discouragement as a temporary loss of perspective. We cannot lose perspective but must trust the Lord for the grace to press on in full belief of His extraordinary promises and stated purposes in connection to prayer. Al Toledo, pastor of The Chicago Tabernacle, reminds us that "the commitment of the few can secure the blessing for the many."[11] Toledo's father-in-law, Jim Cymbala, emphasizes,

"Many churches either pray down heaven's blessing or gradually turn to shallow formulaic methods instead of the living God. But we should not give up or look for shortcuts."[12]

In church life, prayer is not the only thing we do but it must be the first thing we do. It can become the very environment of the ministry. It must be our first resolve not our last resort if our work is to be marked by the unmistakable power of the Holy Spirit. And this will take years, even decades. It will not be easy, but it will be worth it.

In Their Own Words

Watch Pastor Mark Vroegop (College Park Church, Carmel, IN) share his conviction about "Steady Leadership in Prayer" and the power of an Acts 6:4 focus at http://www.64fellowship.com/oldpaths/14/

We shall never see much change for the better in our church in general till the prayer meeting occupies a higher place in the esteem of Christians.[1]

CHARLES SPURGEON

Now, prayer, in order to be continued for any length of time in any other than a formal manner, requires, generally speaking, a measure of strength or godly desire, and the season, therefore, when this exercise of the soul can be most effectually performed is after the inner man has been nourished by meditation on the Word of God, where we find our Father speaking to us, to encourage us, to comfort us, to instruct us, to humble us, to reprove us.[2]

GEORGE MUELLER

7

How to Lead Life-Giving Prayer Experiences

After decades of pastoral ministry, leading multiple prayer meetings every week, I have concluded that God is not the author of boredom, especially when we are conversing with Him. Yet I have been in prayer meetings (and even led some) where participants snored, snorted, drooled, and fell over, while taking a prayer nap. In my book *PRAYzing! An A to Z Guide to Creative Prayer,* I declare war on sleepy prayer times.

If prayer lacks creativity, energy, and innovation, it is not God's fault; it is ours.[3] Admittedly, we've all engaged in some *supplication siestas.* Even Peter, James, and John dozed off in the presence of Jesus, first on the Mount of Transfiguration (Luke 9:32) and later on the Mount of Olives (Matt. 26:36–42). Like Jesus' inner circle, our spirit is willing, but our flesh is weak.

In contrast, the New Testament commands us to be watchful, wakeful, and alert in prayer (Eph. 6:18; Col. 4:2; 1 Peter 4:7). As a pastor, my frustration with lethargic, dozy gatherings has motivated me to try to learn more about how to avoid these dead-in-the-water prayer times. Over the years, I have embraced valuable lessons about creative approaches to prayer. There is still much to learn, but this chapter will help us all to avoid nodding off and restore the old path priority of becoming a praying church.

HOW *NOT* TO START A PRAYER TIME

The opening moments of any prayer gathering often set the trajectory for the entire experience. How we start the prayer time is a core factor in its effectiveness.

"Does anyone have any prayer requests?" I admit that over the years I've heard it and said it. But don't start here. This establishes an immediate man-centered—rather than God-centered—experience. It also eats into time. After Uncle Charlie, Aunt Matilda, and Billy Bob share a long list of ailing body parts, friends traveling on vacation, and third-cousins in crises five states away, no one else has the time or desire to unload all their needs. Time is limited and precious. Of course, this starting point is not a good stewardship of time in any case, because after participants have described in detail all the assortment of needs, we circle back and pray about it all again (if there is any time left actually to pray).

Another traditional approach is to begin by saying, "Let's just pray as we feel led." The intention, I suppose, is an urging to be led by the Spirit in our prayers. Somehow, this gets lost in translation and is interpreted, "Just pray whatever comes to your mind." What ensues is typically a disconnected flurry of impulses based on the experience of the day or pressing frustration of the moment. Not a good place to start.

Commonly, we might even announce, "Let's just pray around the circle." This is unhelpful as participants are forced to pray because it is "their turn" whether the Spirit is really prompting them or not. Introverts freeze up, especially when the person just before them in the circle extrapolates a prolonged King-James-style prayer speech. Of course, if you are the last person in the circle, you either agree with all that has been said since everyone has already stolen your prayer material, or you try to develop some additional content so as not to appear unspiritual.

In Their Own Words

Watch as pastor and prayer facilitator Dennis Fuqua gives practical wisdom on leading prayer and why "All Prayers are not Created Equal" at http://www.64fellowship.com/resources/oldpaths/15/

THE EIGHT GUIDING PRINCIPLES FOR LEADING LIFE-GIVING PRAYER EXPERIENCES

How do we avoid a false start? What are the keys to launching and sustaining a dynamic prayer experience? Here are eight guidelines that can help leaders facilitate prayer. These principles have become very instinctive for me while leading prayer experiences over the years. I am confident you will find them to be effective in many prayer settings: a weekly prayer group, a small group in a home, a Sunday school class, a ministry leadership meeting, and even in large group prayer gathering.

1. Foundation

Begin corporate prayer times (and personal times as well) with an open Bible. This serves as the foundation for prayer. I call this Scripture-fed prayer.

I've noticed in normal interactions that whoever starts a conversation tends to direct the conversation. Prayer is two-way conversation; so who should start the conversation? This depends on our understanding of true prayer. If prayer is our opportunity to blow into God's presence and inform Him of all He needs to do to structure the universe according to our specifications for a happy and comfortable life—then we should start the conversation.

Instead, if prayer is about knowing His will, trusting His grace, and joining Him in His purposes, then we should let Him start the conversation. This requires open Bibles.

Addressing this very idea, Pastor John Piper notes, "I have seen that those whose prayers are most saturated with Scripture are generally most fervent and most effective in prayer. And where the mind isn't brimming with the Bible, the heart is not generally brimming with prayer."[4] George Mueller (the renowned man of faith and evangelist who cared for thousands of orphans and established dozens of Christian schools in the 1800s) spoke about the vital role of Scripture in his prayer life. He noted that for years he tried to pray without starting in the Bible in the morning. Inevitably, his mind wandered sometimes for ten, fifteen, even thirty minutes.[5] Then, when he began to start each morning with the Bible to nourish his soul, he found his heart being transformed by the truth, resulting in spontaneous prayers of confession, thanksgiving, intercession, and supplication. This became his daily experience for decades, resulting in great personal growth and power for life and ministry.

2. Fervor

Fervor is the element of Spirit-led prayer apart from which prayer is impossible. While we know this, we cannot forget the vital, practical role of the Spirit in our united prayers. It is imperative to engage in an intentional focus and reliance upon the Holy Spirit at the outset of every prayer experience. We know He is our indwelling prayer tutor who leads us in prayer that is God-aligned and reassuring—and that ultimately conforms us to Christ and leads to God's glory (see Rom. 8:26–30).

3. Faith

A worship-based faith transforms the nature of all united prayer. Hebrews 11:6 reminds us, "Without faith it is impossible to please him, for whoever would draw near to God must believe that he exists and that he rewards those who seek him." This vital requirement of faith-filled worship in prayer focuses on the reality and character of God, knowing He rewards those who seek Him. Don't miss that focus. Seeking Him, not just presenting long lists of needs, means pursuing His face first and foremost to know His nature.

4. Focus

After we establish this Scripture-fed, Spirit-led, worship-based prayer, we must lead with a biblical and balanced focus. Jesus gave the clear pattern in what has been called the Lord's Prayer. This is not just something to be quoted by memory but to be experienced by corporate enjoyment. (Notice all the plural pronouns.)

> Pray then like this: "Our Father in heaven, hallowed be your name. Your kingdom come, your will be done, on earth as it is in heaven. Give us this day our daily bread, and forgive us our debts, as we also have forgiven our debtors. And lead us not into temptation, but deliver us from evil." (Matt. 6:9–13)

When Jesus said, "Pray like this," it was not just a suggestion or one of many options. It was a command for our good and His glory as we pray. We are not permitted to freelance with traditional alternative approaches or override this model with our own clever "improvements."

In following this pattern, I see a very simple approach but then also a more comprehensive experience. Most fundamentally, there are two parts to the prayer. The first half is entirely Godward (or upward). The second half is manward (or downward). I like to capture this two-part rhythm with this descriptor: "He is worthy. We are needy." Even when there is only a short amount of time to pray, starting with a passage of Scripture then engaging in a pure articulation of worship captures the participants with His worthiness. Then, moving to a time of trusting Him with our needs is natural. Our requests are informed and inspired by our worship.

A more comprehensive breakdown of the prayer is focused on four movements. I describe them as *reverence, response, requests*, and *readiness*, what I called "The 4/4 Pattern for Prayer." This 4/4 pattern, following the exact themes of the model prayer, looks like this:

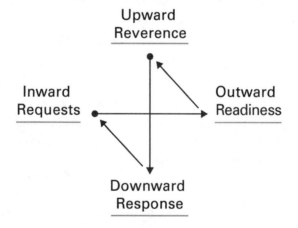

THE 4/4
PATTERN FOR PRAYER

With an open Bible, the beginning point in prayer is to ask, "Who is God?" and "What does He reveal about Himself in this passage?" This sparks worship (reverence) in alignment with the focus, "Our Father in heaven, hallowed be your name."

Since worship is the response of all I am to the revelation of all He is, the next movement is an expression of surrender and submission. "Your kingdom come, your will be done, on earth as it is in heaven" guides to us yield our will, our mind, and our agenda to His purposes. This is prompted by the question, "How do You want me to respond?" and is often guided by a verse in the passage.

"Give us this day our daily bread, and forgive us our debts, as we also have forgiven our debtors" answers the question, "What should we pray about?" Participants can allow the Scripture to guide their requests in connection to both resource needs and relationship needs, as Jesus' model prayer indicates.

In the final movement we find a focus on readiness for spiritual battle. Where do we go from here? What will we face today in a sinful and hostile world? As the pattern indicates, "And lead us not into temptation, but deliver us from evil." Praying from the Scriptures is especially vital at this point, as the best way to overcome the attacks of the enemy is with the memorized and spoken Word of God (Matt. 4:1–10; Eph. 6:17).[6]

5. Flow

The real challenge in leading a prayer time is to facilitate the participation of the people so that all things are done for edification. Sometimes this can feel like herding squirrels. To guide a flow of prayer that reflects continuity, agreement, unity, and blessing I follow what I call "the ABCs of prayer."

Audible. This seems so elementary, but participants must be reminded to pray loudly enough that others can hear. In group prayer, there is no point in opening one's mouth if the others cannot hear. And—we need to hear what the Spirit is prompting in others. Hearing another believer as he prays enables me to know his heart in a deeper way and prompts things in me that I need to pray about. It fosters a collective sense of understanding and agreement. It can even teach me to pray more effectively, especially when the other person is further down the road in their walk with Christ.

Brief. I've been in many prayer times when I wanted to tap someone on the shoulder and ask, "Does your train of thought have a caboose or not?" Long, protracted, scattered prayers have a way of sucking the life out of a prayer time. Encourage brevity on a regular basis. Violators may need to be encouraged offline toward a more measured participation. Many people in prayer meetings are spiritually sincere, just not socially aware.

Clear. Guiding participants to pray clearly, about one thing at a time, encourages greater agreement and focus. When someone dumps a load of thirty-four different requests, it creates confusion as the others do not know which one of the many disconnected appeals to agree with. An effectively led prayer time allows people to pray multiple times but preferably about one thing at time.

Providing distinct entry points helps facilitate this. Also, www.64fellowship.com has many examples of this idea of praying from the Scriptures with balanced focus and edifying continuity.

6. Freedom (to Move and Change Position)

Too many times we lead prayer experiences where participants sit comfortably in a padded chair or pew, with head bowed and eyes closed. This posture can be a surefire recipe for drifting minds and sleeping bodies. It is helpful to give permission (even encouragement) to participants to stand, walk, kneel, or even lay prostrate. Eyes can be opened—and should be when praying from the Scriptures. "You can lift your hands, sit on your hands, clap your hands, look at your hands, and even smell your hands, whatever," I tell people. Just stay physically engaged to allow the body to transmit the expression of the soul.

7. Flexibility

Over the years, with the Lord's help, I have created thousands of Scripture-fed prayer guides that were utilized in corporate prayer gatherings. However, we know that while the Spirit can direct ahead of time He also prompts the unanticipated focus in the moment. The point is simply to prayerfully and thoughtfully plan, as necessary, but to hold the plan loosely, knowing there is a unique dynamic that occurs when believers get together and pray.

8. Faithfulness

Leading in prayer is a lifelong calling, not a short-term fix or the theme of the month. We must embrace a mindset of leading for the long haul. I remember a number of years ago, after more than a decade of intense prayer leadership, crying out to the Lord, "How long do I have to keep up this 'prayer thing'?" In a clear way, the Lord directed my heart to a penetrating question, challenging me to endurance: "Daniel, how long will you brush your teeth, take a shower, eat breakfast, and get dressed?" I understood. It was as if the Lord said, "Why would you question the longevity of this paramount commitment any more than these other basic lifelong routines?" That settled it for me.

Since then, I resolved that the consistent pursuit of spiritual intimacy and leadership in prayer ministry is my way of life until my final day on earth. I tell leaders everywhere I go that they need to develop a dream of dying on their knees. My dream, and I hope yours as well, is to seek spiritual intimacy at a personal level and lead God's people humbly into His presence until my concluding day. Like Paul, let us finish the course!

KEYS TO FACILITATING EFFECTIVE
AND EDIFYING GROUP PARTICIPATION

Beyond these guidelines, here are a couple of practical ways to improve the corporate prayer experience.

Allow for Variety of Participation

While praying out loud brings positive benefit, I never require people to pray aloud. Being a strong extrovert, I do not understand it, but some people get exceedingly stressed over the idea of articulating what is in their hearts in the company of other people.

I like to get people praying together, sometimes in pairs, triplets, or other groupings. However, I always allow the freedom for someone to simply pray alone or exclusively with a spouse or friend with whom they feel more comfortable.

Level the Praying Ground

When praying from the Scriptures, I love to give people a track to run on. The goal is to guide the group in praying with as much specificity and application as possible. Accordingly, you can offer specific entry points that allow people to finish the sentence or fill in the blank. Helping the participants consider specific reasons, times, or circumstances is often a very encouraging tool. Various phrases are effective, such as: because, when, even though, even if, etc.

For example, you might offer any of the following prayer expressions to launch individuals into prayer:

"Lord, thank You that You were faithful when . . ." (Responses might include expressions like:)

- You woke me up this morning to a new day to trust You (Lam. 3:22–23).

- You empowered me to overcome my addiction to drugs (1 Cor. 10:13).
- You forgave and cleansed after a season of rebellion during my college years (1 John 1:9).
- You empowered me to finish my schooling in spite of my weariness (Phil. 1:6).

"Lord, You are great because You are . . ." (Possible responses:)

- You are the creator of the universe (Gen. 1:1).
- You have done awesome deeds throughout history (Ps. 145:5).
- You number and name the stars of heaven (Ps.147:4).
- You are the King of kings and Lord of lords (Rev. 19:16).

"Thank You that You love me, even though . . ."

- I have sinned against You so often (Romans 5:8).
- I often do not even comprehend Your great love (Eph. 3:19).
- I do not act in sacrificial love toward my family and friends (1 John 3:16).

"I am feeling fearful about _____; give me grace to trust You."

"I pray for my friend _____, that I would see him or her come to saving faith."

"Give me faith to share the Gospel this week when . . ."

"My friend, _____, needs your special grace because . . ."

The options are endless, especially when the prompters come right from the truths of Scripture. While this may seem simplistic, the net effect is that it "levels the praying ground." Long-winded people who struggle to find their punctuation are guided to pray specific, focused prayers. This may also enable introverts to participate without feeling that they have to come up with some highly conceptual prayer speech. Such open-ended expressions can help long-term believers to be more transparent and practical in their prayers. New believers find it easy to join in with these simple points of guidance.

SUFFICIENT WORD AND SPIRIT

Beyond these practical recommendations, remember that the Word and Spirit are fully sufficient to equip us to pray and to lead others in prayer. Senior pastor Cliff Boone of Cedar Crest Bible Fellowship Church (Allentown, Pennsylvania) is a champion of expository preaching. Recently he has been awakened to the equal priority of prayer. Cliff told one interviewer, "How could I have missed the priority the Scripture gives to corporate prayer? Now, I never feel more like a pastor than after I have led my people in a prayer meeting. That had been a missing piece of ministry for many years. Before, as I led my people in prayer I always felt inadequate, but now I say, 'This is going to be great. It's a whole new ballgame.'[7] Boone testifies that the blanks have been filled in and speaks of his constant two-part prayer, "Lord, teach me to pray and teach me to teach my people how to pray." This is pastoring as it ought to be in the old paths of "prayer and the ministry of the word."[8]

In Their Own Words

Watch Cliff Boone (Cedar Crest Bible Fellowship Church, Allentown, PA) share his joy about "Learning to Lead in Corporate Prayer" at http://www.64fellowship.com/oldpaths/16/

Prayer is the master-weapon. We should be greatly wise if we used it more, and did so with a more specific purpose.[1]

CHARLES SPURGEON

I believe the greatest indictment on our generation of pastors and Christian leaders is the loss of confidence in calling our people to regular times of corporate prayer. The consequence is a church and leadership that have put their confidence in the wisdom of men, not the promise of God. God is too slow for our taste. It is easier to find the right talent, the right music or program, and give the people what they *think* they need rather than wait on God for what they *really* need . . . Him![2]

PASTOR SANDY MASON

8

A New Movement of Praying Churches

I sat in the back of the magnificent auditorium of The Brooklyn Tabernacle, surrounded by hundreds of other pastors. Like me, they had come to the church to enjoy a two-day conference, hosted by Pastor Jim Cymbala. Over the years, my journey in prayer had converged with Pastor Jim's as I had visted the Tuesday night prayer meeting on many occasions. More recently, he had taught at my church, and I had also been privileged to speak at The Brooklyn Tabernacle.

But in this moment, my eyes scanned the eager assembly of my ministry colleagues from across the country. I realized that soon we would all go home and re-enter the grind of pastoral ministry. The inspiration of these days would likely subside. I knew before long we would all feel disconnected from this wonderful camaraderie and many would become discouraged in the effort that leads to a truly praying church.

As the burden of this reality grew, the Holy Spirit prompted me with several important questions, like:

- What would it take for prayer to truly become an authentic mainstream reality in the churches of our nation?

- How can we help one another to overcome the common discouragement that we face in trying to mobilize prayer in our congregations?
- How can praying pastors connect to one another to provide mutual help and equipping in effective and enduring prayer?

It hit me that whatever captures the attention of pastors tends to drive the agenda of the church. Seemingly, in the current environment, pastors are usually captivated by:

(1) Their denominational efforts, which clearly have value but can soon get lost in bureaucracy and tend to be exclusive and separate from other vital connections to the broader body of Christ;

(2) Megachurch models that offer formulas for ministry success but seldom really transfer into the fabric of that average local church (for a variety of reasons); and/or

(3) Coalitions that seek to connect and motivate pastors around causes like improved evangelism, better small groups, enhanced technology, and distinct theological positions.

The burden of that moment felt like heartburn after a five-course Italian feast. I knew there needed to be a cross-denominational fellowship of praying pastors whose passion was Spirit sent. Such a coalition would not require a superstar leader; it could simply evolve as a network of pastors who, in a spirit of mutual prayer and support, were committed to helping one another make and keep a serious commitment to "prayer and the ministry of the word" as described in Acts 6:4—and throughout the story of the early church.

In subsequent conversations with Pastor Cymbala he affirmed that this was the single greatest need among pastors today. He committed to serve as one of the national co-chairs of this fellowship. Within a year, dozens of pastors gathered in Houston to sign a covenant. The vision of this fellowship would be clear and simple: "to facilitate a Christ-exalting reawakening of pastors to the sufficiency of the Spirit of God, the Word of God, and the people of God through a return to the leadership priorities of Acts 6:4."[3]

ACTS 6:4 THROUGH NEW EYES

My conviction about this approach to pastoral leadership emerged early in my own pastoral ministry when it seemed that I saw this Acts 6 passage through new eyes. While I had read Acts 6:4 and its surrounding verses many previous times, the Spirit that day made fresh application to my heart. *Prayer* and the ministry of the Word.

I realized I had seven solid years of formal training in "the ministry of the word" and many other related topics. I had been required to take classes in hermeneutics, homiletics, hamartiology, eschatology, pneumatology, soteriology, and ecclesiology along with many Old and New Testament classes, punctuated by studies in the original languages. All of this underscored the priority of the Scriptures. Yet virtually nothing in my ministry preparation gave meaningful (and certainly not equal) priority to the ministry of prayer. I recalled Jesus' declaration: "My house shall be called a house of prayer for all the nations" (Mark 11:17).

The subtle message for many of us in this approach to education has been that prayer is just "assumed" or it really is not that important after all. One major seminary actually had a "chair of prayer" for many years. When the lead professor retired, the school chose not to renew this commitment with the explanation that "prayer is just not an academic topic and we are an academic institution."

I understand the academic mindset, but nowhere in the Bible are we told that education and degrees are the secret to effective Gospel ministry. Education is a vital ingredient and it is wise to have an adequate toolbox for effective church ministry. Yet tools without power are about as useful as a chain saw with no gasoline.

Tozer said it this way,

> No man should stand before an audience who has not first stood before God. Many hours of communion should precede one hour in the pulpit. The prayer chamber should be more familiar than the public platform. Prayer should be continuous, preaching but intermittent. . . . It is significant that the schools teach everything about preaching except the important part, praying. . . . That it is the one religious work which gets done with the least enthusiasm, cannot but be one of the tragedies of our times.[4]

WHERE DO WE GO?

So where do pastors get the equipping to lead a church in prayer? How do we really develop a pervasive culture of prayer in our churches? How do we discover the principles for shaping a praying leadership team? These are some of the questions The 6:4 Fellowship seeks to satisfy as we connect, encourage, and equip pastors.

My training came from "the school of hard knocks." My very patient and relentless professor was the Holy Spirit. My textbook was the Word of God. My willing classmates were the faithful praying people in my churches. In many ways, my mentor was Jim Cymbala, both from afar and eventually in a personal fashion. Over time, the Lord helped me lead effectively, and we saw thousands of lives transformed in prayer.

But let's be honest. If prayer is really so clear in the Bible and was so vital to the power of the early church, should we not be more intentional in emphasizing it and provide more equipping toward that end? Should this not be a primary emphasis in our efforts to encourage one another in ministry? Should it not be a major emphasis and experience in all of our regional and national leadership conferences, over and above new strategies, programs, and formulas for ministry advancement? Yet, prayer is typically marginalized when the leaders gather to be inspired and trained.

One CEO and the main speaker for a national prison ministry recalls attending a major pastors' conference a few years ago; its theme was "The Powerful Prayer

> *Prayer is typically marginalized when the leaders gather to be inspired and trained.*

Life of a Praying Pastor." He noted almost two thousand pastors and ministry leaders attended the three-day conference, which included singing, preachers lecturing about the importance of prayer, and "stories of the prayer lives of those considered the giants of the faith." After Manny Mill returned home he realized, "Not once were we ever called to pray! No time was scheduled for corporate prayer. No one encouraged us from the front to consider skipping a meal . . . to pray individually or with others." Then Mill added, "There was a prayer room opened throughout the conference, as was the custom each year. But the few times I visited the room to pray, only one or two others were present."[5]

Whether it's at a leadership conference or pastors' meeting, this lack of focus on prayer in our churches and among our pastors is telling. Cymbala nails it when he writes:

> How can we really believe in the Bible—God's Holy Word—while our churches are failing to be houses of prayer? Today in the contemporary church, there seems to be a practical denial

of the efficacy of prayer. It is vital to remember what most have forgotten: God's house is to be called, not a house of preaching, or of worship, or of fellowship, but a house of prayer![6]

In this book, I am seeking to help us detach from the many distractions that keep us from this salient priority. If we can see current ministry through the lens of the old paths of Acts, a new day could emerge. If we could affirm the profound value and proper balance of "prayer and the ministry of the word" we could experience a new reality of Spirit-imparted power. Professor Donald McDougall declared,

> Leaders in the early church brought in other individuals to plan and program so that they might "devote" themselves "to prayer, and to the ministry of the word" (Acts 6:4). By their example they evidence that the two best ways of knowing and yielding to the mind of God are prayer and a commitment to reading, obeying and teaching God's Word without rationalization or reservation. Prayer was and is a major key. To our shame, many of us who are committed to the importance of the ministry of the Word do not have an equal commitment to the importance of prayer.[7]

Redefining Leadership Roles

The three churches to which I was called were led by "elders." They were wonderful, devoted men. But in each case I learned that while they were using a biblical title, significant confusion existed about their biblical role. For the most part, these elders were actually functioning as trustees or deacons, giving more of their time to budgets, buildings, and personnel issues and very little time to "prayer and the ministry of the word."

Through biblical study and group discussion around some key books,[8] we began to define and refine the role of the elders to align with the biblical priorities of "prayer and the ministry of the word." Additional teams were created to take on all of the other administrative items that formerly dominated the meetings, with simple reports back to the elders at the monthly gathering.

Monthly elder meetings that had been comprised of opening prayer, closing prayer, and four to five hours of administrative discussion went away. The new reality involved sixty to ninety minutes of prayer and Scripture, followed by a couple hours of high-level reports, also punctuated by prayer. (See Appendix 3 for a brief biblical summary of the function of elders.)

I witnessed a similar transition at Hill Country Bible Church in Austin, Texas. Tim Hawks became the lead pastor three years after the church began in 1986. In the subsequent thirty years, Hill Country has passionately embraced a mission "that every man, woman and child in Greater Austin has the chance to experience the life-changing reality of Jesus Christ because they hear the Gospel from the lips of someone at Hill Country Bible Church." This has led to a church planting passion that features an intentional and effective training center. As a result, today over twenty-five churches are a part of The Association of Hill Country Bible Churches. I had the joy of consulting with Hill Country for a year, helping to develop a stronger prayer culture.

Prayer has become a core value of Hill Country. For years the elders met weekly from 6:00 a.m. to 8:00 a.m. The old format involved an opening prayer and a closing prayer, bookending a lot of discussion. More recently, they have spent the first hour reflecting on an attribute of God, worshiping in prayer around that truth, and then interceding for the ministry and one another as the Spirit would direct. Their bold testimony is that they get more done in the one hour after extended prayer than they ever did in two hours with perfunctory prayer.[9]

A church will never become a house of prayer until the core leaders become a people of prayer. Returning to a biblical model, rather than a traditional or corporate framework, is a vital foundation.

Maximize Shared Experiences

Leith Anderson has often said, "One of the keys to unity is shared experiences." To strengthen the unity of your core leaders, it is important to pursue shared experiences that will cultivate a conviction and enduring commitment to prayer. Reading books together about prayer and the Word is a great starting place.

But experiences can be much more than reading and discussing books. When I was called to the church in Minnesota, I knew we needed to take some radical steps to ignite a deeper devotion to prayer. Apart from something supernatural I knew that the pain of the violation of trust by my predecessor, the burden of massive debt, and the overall loss of momentum was going to threaten the health and future of the church.

In the early months, I made the decision to charter a 180-passenger plane. The plan was to leave Minneapolis at 6:00 a.m. We would land at JFK Airport, jump on the subway, enjoy lunch at The Brooklyn Tabernacle, meet with Pastor Jim Cymbala and his staff, and then experience the Tuesday night prayer meeting. When I made that commitment I knew my annual salary was on the line.

The Lord helped us fill the plane (for this trip and another one a year later) and the "shared experience" of these days catalyzed a significant work of prayer that made the difference in this difficult season of the church.

Each year, our ministry sponsors a "Day of Renewal" coalescing leaders from across North America for a high-impact day that includes teaching, Q & A, a pastors' luncheon and, of course, the experience of the prayer meeting. The smart pastors always bring others with them.

I would encourage you to find key ways to discover shared

experiences through the reading of books, watching inspiring videos (on the Internet, www.64fellowship.com is packed with these), or attending strategic gatherings together. These might be prayer summits, conferences, or retreats.

Learn from Godly Colleagues

Over the years I have read many books on prayer. On occasion I brought in some speakers who could teach and inspire my church toward greater prayer. As rich as these resources seemed, I realized that very few of these presenters were pastors. If they were pastors, they did not lead a truly praying church, even though they had great prayer content. I wanted to learn from a pastor who not only had insight but was implementing prayer in a significant way in his church. Soon I learned that finding these pastors felt like locating a lost nickel in a hayfield.

A key goal of The 6:4 Fellowship is to make this search easy and these connections life-giving. The Lord is enabling us to identify praying pastors all across the nation. These pastors have not arrived but are making substantive progress and are willing to share their lessons with other colleagues.[10] We believe it is vital to connect pastors to one another, to learn from one another, and to cheer each other ahead in the priorities of "prayer and the ministry of the word."

Connect with Like-Minded Pastors

At a national level, The 6:4 Fellowship facilitates encouraging camaraderie among pastors who share a mutual commitment to "prayer and the ministry of the word." We do this by way of regional and national gatherings, coaching groups, and prayer times via the Internet. Capturing the feel of a holy reunion, pastors learn from one another, find encouragement, and pray together with extraordinary passion.

More organically, the pursuit of vital prayer with other local pastors in your own community can facilitate great personal encouragement and kingdom impact. Movements of united prayer are springing up in cities and towns all across the nation. I've had the privilege of leading multi-day prayer summits in many of these locales. The benefits and challenges of this kind of mutual commitment are many, but the fruit is often profound. (See Appendix 4, "Pastors Praying Together.")

For more than twenty years pastors in Austin have been meeting every month in small groups across the city. They call these gatherings "Pastors in Covenant" (PIC) Groups. Their camaraderie in prayer has led to a united passion they describe as "In the City for The City." Beyond nurturing positive soul care for the pastors individually, these prayer groups are uniting for a greater collective impact, all birthed in prayer. In some years, pastors across the city have even preached concurrent series as an expression of their united passion. I've had the joy of consulting with some of the Austin churches in recent years and also of leading their annual Pastors' Prayer Summit, where hundreds of these pastors come for united prayer and worship to deepen their relationships and fuel their mission in the region.

In Their Own Words

Watch Pastor Tim Hawks (Hill Country Bible Church, Austin, TX) talk about the profound effect of pastors praying together at http://www.64fellowship.com/oldpaths/17/

UNITY IN KATY

For more than twenty years (since 1995) the pastors of Katy, Texas, have prayed together every Wednesday at noon. This commitment emerged from the prayers for revival burning in the heart of

Pastor Charles Wisdom of the First Baptist Church. As he prayed, he sensed the Lord asking him, "Charles, would you be okay if I brought revival to the Methodist Church instead? Or to the Episcopal Church?" This prodding led Pastor Wisdom to realize that God's heart for revival was not focused exclusively on his church or his denomination. (I often note that we all want revival, as long as it starts in our denomination.) For these two decades, Charles has been a catalyst to united prayer in Katy. Jim Leggett, senior pastor of Grace Fellowship (see the Old Path Profile at the end of this section), has spoken openly on how praying together has empowered all of the churches to increase in their Gospel impact in a way that far exceeds the growth of one single megachurch.

In one email, Pastor Leggett described how eighty pastors gathered at their most recent prayer summit. Next year they expect four hundred pastors as the churches in greater Houston have asked to join in. More than three thousand people attended their most recent National Day of Prayer citywide event. This was followed by fifty straight hours of prayer and worship, Leggett reported.[11]

From this common passion for the lost, the churches in Katy and the greater Houston area have united together in consistent Gospel efforts that have reached countless lives.[12] This has also brought new spiritual vibrancy to each local congregation. These praying pastors are leading praying churches. A new heart for the lost has increased the mission focus of the local congregations.

In Their Own Words

Watch Gbolahan Faluade (River of Life Family Church, Katy, TX) share his "Passion for Praying with Other Pastors" at http://www.64fellowship.com/oldpaths/18/

UNITED IN TITUSVILLE

In recent years, Titusville, Florida, has experienced a serious economic downturn as the Space Shuttle program was discontinued by NASA. (Located adjacent to the Kennedy Space Center, Titusville has been significantly dependent on the space program for decades.) This crisis prompted the pastors to begin praying together for an hour every Wednesday. As of this writing, more than forty pastors gather weekly for "Scripture-fed, Spirit-led, worship-based prayer." They testify that they have all learned to pray more powerfully in their own lives as a result of praying together.

D. A. Carson has affirmed this dynamic, "Many facets of Christian discipleship, not the least prayer, are more effectively passed on by modeling than from teaching. Good praying is more easily caught than taught. . . . We should choose models from whom we can learn."[13]

This "learning" has led to dynamic spiritual health in the hearts of the pastors and in their churches. Not surprisingly, their organic unity has ignited several key initiaitives that have elevated the Gospel and led to practical initiatives in serving the needy in the city.

JOIN THE INITIATIVE

It was Matthew Henry, referring to revival, who said "When God intends great mercy for His people, the first thing He does is set them a-praying."[14] I believe the fact that you are reading this right now is part of God's intention to pour out a great mercy on your life and church. The 6:4 Fellowship, and other efforts like it, are all part of a divine initiative to call us back to the old paths so that we might experience a new power for the sake of the Gospel. The stories of the Lord stirring leaders to pray together in such extraordinary ways are a precursor of things to come. The next steps of "prayer and the word" in your congregation represent your cooperation with the heart and plan of Christ to exalt His name for the sake of the lost. In response to this divine proposal, may our cry remain, "Lord, teach us to pray."

ON THE PATH TO POWER

Contemporary America and a Call to Prayer
BY JOHN PIPER

I would like to call us to new passion in prayer.

Let prayer rise among all our priorities, and permeate all our activities, to the degree that our goals are impossible for humans to achieve. What would that include?

All *conversions to Christ* are impossible for humans to achieve. Jesus said so, when the rich young ruler turned away: "With man this is impossible, but with God all things are possible" (Matt. 19:26).

All *holy living* is impossible for humans to achieve. This is because holy living is by definition "walking by the Spirit" (Gal. 5:16), and "by the Spirit you put to death the deeds of the body" (Rom. 8:13). If the Spirit does not come in power, we cannot live holy lives.

Or another way to say it is that *faith* is impossible for humans to produce without God's life-giving power (Eph. 2:8); and whatever is not from faith is sin (Rom. 14:23); and "without faith it is impossible to please [God]" (Heb. 11:6). Therefore, all God-pleasing, non-sinning life is impossible for mere humans.

God has appointed faith-driven prayer as the normal way for us to receive what we cannot achieve. "You do not have, because you do not ask" (James 4:2). "Call upon me in the day of trouble; I will deliver you, and you shall glorify me" (Ps. 50:15).

God's judgments are already falling heavily on America. "Since they did not see fit to acknowledge God, God gave them up to a debased mind to do what ought not to be done" (Rom. 1:28). Without a deep and pervasive awakening of Christ-exalting faith and holiness, this judgment will climax in a cataclysm of physical and cultural destruction.

There is reason to believe that God's judgment begins with His house. "It is time for judgment to begin at the household of God; and if it begins with us, what will be the outcome for those who do not obey the gospel of God?" (1 Peter 4:17). The call for cultural awakening includes the call for *Christian* reformation and revival.

This awakening and reformation and revival is impossible for humans to bring about. Only God can turn the hearts of millions of people from the love of sin to the love of Christ.

Therefore, I appeal to pastors and church members alike: Let us move to a new level in our commitment to pray for the outpouring of God's saving and sanctifying power in our day.

- Set aside new time alone with God to ask him for omnipotent intervention in the awakening of Christ-exalting faith and holiness.
- Find a few like-minded friends and arrange to meet weekly for thirty minutes or one hour, where you do not discuss anything or share prayer requests, but only pray. Someone reads a passage of Scripture and the remaining twenty-eight (or fifty-eight) minutes are dedicated to prayer. Then get up and go back to your work.

- Build a season of prayer into every church gathering. Not an opening prayer only, but a "season" of prayer. That is what the first half of our worship services is as we sing our prayers. I am saying let *all* other gatherings be soaked with a season that says: What matters most here cannot happen without divine intervention.

- Let every speaker at every Christian conference be prayed over by the conference leaders for at least fifteen minutes. Don't send a man or woman to speak to hundreds and thousands of people without pleading over them that they would be empowered by God that miracles would happen, because the miracle of conversion and holiness is what we live for.

- Let pastors' gatherings be transformed, so that there is enough prayer that all feel: We acted as if what we really want could not happen without the intervention of the prayer-hearing God.

- Let every pastor ask the Lord: Is it time for me to take unusual leadership to summon my people, and the networks I am part of, to extraordinary prayer?

When Jesus looked out on the crowds who "were harassed and helpless, like sheep without a shepherd" (Matt. 9:36), he called his disciples to pray. I echo that call.

Adapted from "A Contemporary America and a Call to Prayer"; http://www.desiringgod.org/articles/contemporary-america-and-a-call-to-prayer. Used by permission.

AN OLD PATHS PROFILE
PASTOR JIM LEGGETT

IN 1996, PASTOR JIM LEGGETT launched Grace Fellowship in Katy, Texas. Today the church reaches thousands every week, yet Grace is anything but a typical megachurch. Its stated vision is to become "A House of Prayer for All Nations." Its impact through prayer is truly extraordinary.

The church itself was birthed in a profound prayer effort. More than four hundred people at its mother church prayed daily for six months. Prior to the launch of the church ninety-six people engaged in a seven-week prayer and fasting vigil. This was matched with twelve Sunday night prayer gatherings leading up to the launch. In addition, twenty-two people conducted a prayer walk of the community, praying for thousands of households in the neighborhoods where the church would start.

Leggett describes the results simply as a testimony to the power of God and what He does when He moves His people to pray. In the past twenty years the church has conducted dozens of internal prayer campaigns. It has an extensive budget for prayer and a full staff team. At the same time the church dedicated a large space to what is known as the Great SouthWest Prayer Center, a center established for the city of Katy and the greater Houston region (see http://thegreatsouthwestprayercenter.org.

Leggett firmly believes that the prayer ministry must begin at the pastoral level, then must be prioritized with time, money, energy, staff, and square footage.

Today, Grace Fellowship has more than five hundred volunteers actively engaged in prayer ministry on a regular basis, ministering to God through their "Audience of One" (24/7 worship and intercession), meeting to pray together, or ministering to others personally or on the phone. Each year, thousands receive prayer through the prayer phone line, at the end of the services, and through other specialized intercessory efforts. During one National Day of Prayer more than four thousand people came to worship and intercede from across the city of Katy. In a recent "Fire on the Altar" event, more than one thousand came over several days with multiple churches participating in a three-day prayer service.

As noted in chapter 8, the pastors of Katy have been meeting weekly for prayer every Wednesday morning for more than twenty years.

Brenda Martin, a full-time staff member who coordinates the prayer efforts at Grace Fellowship, calculated that the impact in one twelve-month period was that 38,394 specific prayers were offered—affecting the city, the nation, people groups, kingdoms, and continents.

She describes the result as the exaltation of Jesus in the belief that every nation, tongue, and tribe will know and worship Jesus, for the glory of God.

"Perhaps a key missing link in many churches in America is grasping the importance of a corporate abiding in Christ as a local church," Martin says. "Placing Christ in the driver's seat of the local church happens as we surrender control of the church to Jesus, especially through corporate praying and prayer ministries."

PART 3

PREACHING LEADERS AND THE SUFFICIENCY OF THE TRUTH OF GOD

Is it not clear as you take a bird's eye view of Church history, that the decadent periods and eras in the history of the Church have always been those periods when preaching had declined? What is it that always heralds the dawn of a Reformation or of a Revival? It is renewed preaching.[1]

MARTYN LLOYD-JONES

In many instances modern preaching seems to fail in the very thing which should create and distinguish true preaching, which is essential to its being, and which alone can make of it a divine and powerfully aggressive agency. It lacks, in short, "the power from on high" which alone can make it a living thing. It fails to become the channel through which God's saving power can be made to appeal to men's consciences and hearts.[2]

E. M. BOUNDS

9

Preaching with Understanding, Unction, and Utterance

I remember sitting in chapel at Liberty Baptist College (now Liberty University) as a sophomore pastoral major. An unlikely presenter was preaching that day. He was an insurance executive and live-wire inspirational speaker named Charles Tremendous Jones. Midway through his message he made a statement that so caught my attention I later rubbed a few nickels together and bought the cassette tape recording (for those of you old enough to remember cassettes). I replayed a section of Jones's message until I had written down his statement.

Decades later, I can still quote it: "All the truth in the world will do you little good until God brings a man across your path, and you are able to see that truth in action. Then, suddenly, that truth becomes a driving force in your life."

When it comes to preaching, God has blessed me with many incarnations of "truth in action." I was saved under the dynamic evangelistic preaching of my older brother, Dennis, now a pastor in Oklahoma. My father-in-law, Fred Brewer (now in heaven), was a senior pastor for fifty years. Later he served as the pastor to senior adults under David Jeremiah. When he preached, he was articulate and passionate. His deep blue eyes seemed to burn like fire when he spoke.

My brother-in-law, Vernon Brewer, is a dynamic preacher. As the president of a mission organization called World Help, he preaches all around the world. His zeal for the needs of the unreached masses inspires like no other. After surviving cancer, enduring eighteen surgeries in eighteen months, the intensity and impact of his preaching has accelerated.

But I have two mentors who have crossed my path and most influenced my conviction about the primacy of "the ministry of the word." Both are as different from the other as the ocean shore is from the mountain top. Each has shaped my understanding of preaching in unique ways. The first is John MacArthur; the second, Jim Cymbala. (You probably never expected to hear those two names in the same sentence.)

I've also been marked by the prayer of Dr. Lee Toms, my forty-year predecessor at the church I served in Sacramento, California. He often pleaded with the Lord, "God give me understanding, unction, and utterance." This trilogy of foci has never left me. And it is the theme of this chapter.

UNDERSTANDING

In my late twenties I joined the staff at Grace Community Church in Sun Valley, California, to serve as John MacArthur's associate pastor and personal assistant. As I worked at my desk most days, handling correspondence, meeting with staff, and coordinating John's schedule, he was in the office next door in earnest study. On occasions he would call me into his study and ask my opinion about a particular text or topic in connection with his upcoming sermon. Of course, this was tantamount to the chief pilot of a

747 asking a kid with a paper airplane how to fly. I am not sure I ever offered anything of consequence. In those sacred moments of treasured interaction in the inner-chamber of his study, I gained a profound sense of his heartfelt, holy dedication to understanding the text.

The Commitment to Understanding

Dr. MacArthur has often said that the secret to great preaching is simply to keep your rear end in the chair until the sermon is done. Diligent, disciplined, determined study has marked his ministry for more than five decades.

Pastor and seminary professor Arturo Azurdia writes about the steadfastness of the early apostles to refuse to "serve tables" when confronted with the demands of feeding the neglected widows. They resolved, "It is not desirable that we should leave the word of God" (Acts 6:2 NKJV). We know they delegated the leadership of this feeding task to seven spiritually qualified men.

"Does this delegation reflect laziness on the part of the original apostles?" Azurdia asks, "Worse yet, does it betray a sense of spiritual superiority on their parts? No, it is nothing but a division of labor that seeks to protect the centrality of preaching in God's design."[3]

Recall the apostle Paul's compelling description of the primary characteristic of elders who are worthy of double honor. They "labor in preaching and teaching" (1 Tim. 5:17). They work in their study and preaching to the point of exhaustion. The original Greek word means, "To be tired or weary, as the result of hard or difficult endeavor."[4]

Azudia elaborates,

> Preachers (and their congregations!) must understand that faith-
> fulness to God's methodology will, by necessity, exempt them

from significant participation in most other ministry responsibilities. If men such as these, given to preaching and teaching, labor unto weariness in this work, then it is highly unlikely they will have significant involvement with other ministries, however important they may be. Faithful exposition is an all-consuming work; a faithful man is immovable from this design. He recognizes preaching is the method ordained of God.[5]

A commitment to understanding the text ensures accuracy and undergirds authority in preaching.

In Their Own Words

Watch Pastor Brian Lorrits (Trinity Grace Church, New York, NY) talk about "The Power of Memorizing the Text" at http://www.64fellowship.com/oldpaths/19/

The Confidence of Understanding

Our confidence in pursuing a deep understanding of the preached Word is rooted in our certainty about the sufficiency of the Scriptures. MacArthur's diligent study—most often for thirty or more hours a week—is rooted in his high view of Scripture. He writes,

> Scripture alone is the foundation for preaching. In it alone lies the life-giving message of salvation and edification God wants proclaimed from the pulpit. Scripture is the faithful Word, the trustworthy, reliable, dependable Word, in contrast to the untrustworthy, unreliable words of human wisdom. Only in the Scriptures are the mind of God, the will of God, the purpose of God and the plan of God revealed.[6]

When I traveled with John, he took every appropriate opportunity to speak to pastors' gatherings and crowds of radio listeners from Psalm 19:7–11, which expounds the multifaceted beauty of the law, testimonies, precepts, and commandments of the Lord. With integrity and intensity, MacArthur would proclaim, "They are more desirable than gold, yes, than much fine gold; sweeter also than honey and drippings of the honeycomb. Moreover, by them Your servant is warned; in keeping them there is great reward" (vv. 10–11 NASB).

His heart is seen in the following words from *Rediscovering Pastoral Ministry:*

> Scripture alone is the source of spiritual food. Peter urged believers to "long for the pure milk of the word, that by it you may grow in respect to salvation" (1 Peter 2:2). Scripture alone is "able to build [believers] up and to give [them] the inheritance among all those who are sanctified" (Acts 20:32). In Scripture alone is found "the wisdom that leads to salvation through faith which is in Christ Jesus" (2 Timothy 3:15). Scripture alone "is inspired by God and profitable for teaching, for reproof, for correction, for training in righteousness" (2 Timothy 3:16).[7]

His passion bleeds again:

> Preachers must return to their calling as expositors of Scripture. Like Ezra they must "set [their hearts] to study the law of the Lord, and to practice it, and to teach His statutes and ordinances" (Ezra 7:10). Like Apollos, they must strive to be "mighty in the Scriptures" (Acts 18:24). And like Paul, they must realize that they were made ministers "according to the stewardship from God." That they "might fully carry out the preaching of the word of God" (Colossians 1:25). Only then will they recover the proper foundation of preaching.[8]

When Martin Luther described his role in the Reformation, he extolled the sufficiency of the Word of God: "I simply taught, preached, and wrote God's Word; otherwise I did nothing. And while I slept . . . the Word did everything."[9]

AN UNDERGIRDING UNCTION

In recent years, I've been honored to co-lead one-day events for pastors alongside Pastor Jim Cymbala. While Jim did not graduate from seminary, he is profoundly well-read, with an impressive library of classic Christian writing and a wide array of theological works. For many years, he has been mentored through near-weekly conversations with Dr. Warren Wiersbe, former general director of *Back to the Bible* radio.

A Reliance on and Anointing of the Holy Spirit

Several years ago Jim was prompted by the Lord to stop using notes as he preached. By his own testimony, this produced a new level of reliance on the Holy Spirit but also drove him to study the Scriptures even more diligently.

I have often asked Jim on the evening prior to our presentations about his selected text and topic. (He usually speaks first in the morning and I follow prior to lunch.) Every time his answer has been the same, "I don't know yet. I am waiting on the Lord." In his waiting, Jim would spend the evening locked away in his hotel room, seeking direction from the Holy Scriptures and the Holy Spirit.

Jim was seeking what godly men in earlier times called "the unction of the Spirit." *Unction* is a word often associated with the biblical idea of "anointing." In the Old Testament, kings, prophets, and priests were anointed with oil, symbolic of the blessing and power of the Holy Spirit. As we are using it, unction would be best understood as a clear demonstration of the power of the Holy Spirit in and through the life and message of a preacher.

E. M. Bounds described it this way, "Unction makes God's truth powerful and interesting, draws and attracts, edifies, convicts, saves. Unction vitalizes God's revealed truth, makes it living and life-giving. Even God's truth spoken without this unction is light, dead and deadening."[10]

Charles S. Spurgeon underscored this as he equipped ministry students: "One bright [benefit] which private prayer brings down upon the ministry is an indescribably and inimitable something, better understood than named; it is a dew from the Lord, a divine presence which you will recognize at once when I say it is 'an unction from the holy one.'"[11]

Attempts to Manufacture Unction

In his day, Spurgeon watched many of his contemporaries try to manufacture unction with various manipulations. In our day, we try to fabricate impact and life transformation with countless forms of media, high-tech enhancements, and working the crowd with clever technique. More than a century later, and in a world of light-speed change, Spurgeon's words still ring true:

> Some have tried to imitate unction by unnatural tones and whines; by running up the whites of their eyes, and lifting their hands in almost ridiculous manner. . . . Bah! The whole thing smells of the green-room and the stage. The getting up of fervor in hearers by the simulation of it in the preaching is a loathsome deceit to be scorned by honest men. . . . Unction is a thing which you cannot manufacture, and its counterfeits are worse than worthless; yet it is in itself priceless and beyond measure needful if you would edify believers and bring sinners to Jesus. To the secret pleader with God this secret is committed; upon him rest the dew of the Lord, about him is the perfume which makes the heart glad.[12]

Spurgeon's "Bah!" from his observations of his contemporaries would likely be amplified and repeated with exponential passion today. The bodily manipulations of his day have been replaced with sophisticated and scripted techniques for stimulating the congregation with visuals, smoke, lights, irrelevant (and sometimes irreverent) humor, and close-up shots of the performers on the stage to "engage" the crowd. We have replaced spiritual unction with technological function.

We have replaced spiritual unction with technological function.

Azurdia reminds us that these are without sustaining power, for the impact of the Gospel message comes first and foremost from the Holy Spirit:

> The most gifted preacher is impotent to inaugurate a saving experience apart from a gracious work of the omnipotent Spirit. Therefore, any effective ministry of exposition must include both a resolute commitment to the practice of diligent exegesis and a thorough going dependence upon the ministry of the Holy Spirit.[13]

Spurgeon urged, "If the anointing which we bear come not from the Lord of Hosts, we are deceivers, and since only in prayer can we obtain it, let us continue instant, constant, fervent in supplications."[14] Azurdia agrees:

> If the aim of Christian preaching is more than intellectual enlightenment and moral reformation, but is, instead, the thorough-going transformation of people dead in trespasses and sins, then Christian preachers must rest their dependence solely upon the Spirit of the living God because such a transformation requires a power of an altogether supernatural kind. Stated simply, the power of the Holy Spirit is the *sine qua non* of Gospel preaching, the one thing without which nothing else matters.[15]

OUR UNPARALLELED UTTERANCE

Words Given by the Spirit

Most preachers have had at least one parishioner comment on the profound impact of a particular point or phrase in a sermon. The person testifies that it changed their life. In rehearsing the sermon in his head, and even consulting his notes, that pastor has no recollection of making such a statement. How does he explain this? I would bank on the idea of Spirit-empowered utterance in the moments of delivery. Spurgeon said such words come from "celestial hands":

> Most preachers who depend upon God's Spirit will tell you that their freshest and best thoughts are not those which were premeditated, but ideas which come to them, flying as on the wings of angels; unexpected treasure brought on a sudden by celestial hands, seed of the flowers of paradise, wafted from the mountains of myrrh.[16]

Truly our utterance is more than reading from a carefully crafted manuscript. The Holy Spirit works before time and in time; in the study and in the preaching moment. We must be earnest in our expectation of both.

In Their Own Words

Watch Pastor Jeff Schwarzentraub from Harvest Bible Chapel (Denver), as he speaks about the balance of "Biblical-Preparation vs. Spirit-Led Delivery" at http://www.64fellowship.com/oldpaths/20/

"Christianity is not primarily a teaching religion," Cymbala notes. "Christianity is essentially a supernatural religion. . . . Ministers are supposed to lead their congregations into fellowship with God himself and not merely their slant on the truth with innovative props and illustrations."[17] Of course, we need the Lord's grace that we might personally experience a supernatural fellowship with God, certainly as a lifestyle, but particularly before we step into the pulpit and as we impart the living Word.

Prayed-Up to Preach

The Lord taught me this through a routine of prayer that I practiced for more than twenty years. Every Sunday morning, usually very early, I would gather with other willing hearts for an hour or Scripture-fed, Spirit-led, worship-based prayer. We would typically gather at 6:30 and begin by reading a psalm. We would observe the truths about God's works and character, then commence with a free-flowing time of worship. No requests were offered, only spontaneous adoration for Him, even punctuated with a cappella song (although we weren't much of a choir at that time in the morning).

Following this, we would take a few quiet moments to surrender our hearts, thoughts, and agendas to the Holy Spirit. As we began to think about the prayer needs of the day, we would disperse for an individual thirty-minute prayer-walk of the facility. Some would walk through the entire auditorium, praying for each row and the lives of those who would soon be in the services. Some prayed in the lobby, at the entry doors, in the youth rooms, in the children's areas, and on the platform. I would usually end up on my face behind the pulpit, pleading for the empowerment and wisdom of the Holy Spirit for the coming hours.

In the final fifteen minutes everyone would gather in the front. My worship pastors and I would either kneel or sit in the middle as the others circled around. (I explained that we were not more important than others; we were just more desperate.) The final season of prayer was spent claiming the promises, praying for the application of the day's biblical text, and trusting the Lord for great victories. Usually, as this prayer time ended, my worship pastor began his rehearsals. I retreated to my study to prayerfully reflect on what the Lord seemed to be saying in the final moments before the message.

These were some of my most treasured moments of the week. While my notes were already printed, the promptings and insights gained as a result of that environment of prayer were often the most profound. God taught me week-by-week that although the horse was prepared for the day of battle, victory came from the Lord (Prov. 21:31). This enriched my vital understanding of the role of the Holy Spirit in the delivery of the message.

In the preaching moment, there are realities that we cannot script. These are things only the Holy Spirit can know. And it is His sermon, after all. As people assemble, only the Spirit sees the confluence of needs, dilemmas, questions, doubts, and defeats represented in the unique gathering of that moment. His wisdom is able to apply God's Word to the deepest needs. Only the Holy Spirit discerns the sinful secrets of the hearts of those sitting in the crowd in need of the convicting power of the truth. We align our hearts with this great dynamic as we keep a posture of intentional, dependent, and spiritually sensitive prayer.

The letters to the seven churches of Revelation (Rev. 2–3) teach us two important truths. First, the Lord had (and has) a specific message and plan for each church. Second, the key to the application and obedience to that message is found in the seven-times repeated command, "Let him who has ears hear what the Spirit is saying to the churches." The same Spirit who brooded over creation and by whose power the worlds came into being; the same Spirit who inspired the Scriptures; the same Spirit who filled the believers at Pentecost to birth the church—this is the same Spirit who works in the preacher to bring powerful application of His truth to scores, hundreds, even thousands of hearts at the same time in the utterance of the truth of the Gospel.

Ultimate Relevance

Many preachers pursue relevance by spending massive amounts of time reading the latest cultural tabloids and searching the Internet for the cutting-edge trends. Of course, there is value in keeping up with the news and understanding the times. However, ultimate relevance comes from the Holy Spirit who alone knows the real cross section between contemporary issues of the day with the deepest needs of the human heart. The Holy Spirit is the most relevant force in relating the Gospel to the needs and struggles of the human heart. Thus Geoffrey Thomas warns:

> One of the great perils that face preachers . . . is the problem of hyper-intellectualism, that is, the constant danger of lapsing into a purely cerebral form of proclamation, which falls exclusively upon the intellect. Men become obsessed with the doctrine and end up as brain-oriented preachers. There is consequently a fearful impoverishment in their hearts emotionally, devotionally, and practically. . . . It is one thing to explain the truth of Christianity to men and women; it is another thing to feel the overwhelming power of the sheer loveliness and enthrallment of Jesus Christ and to communicate that dynamically to the whole person who listens so that there is a change of such dimensions that he loves Him with his heart and soul and mind and strength.[18]

I've heard it attributed to John Wesley and have kept the quote on my desk in my study for over twenty years, "God's word sets me on fire and people come to see me burn." Understanding. Unction. Utterance. Like sun, moon, and stars are to sky so are these to a burning pulpit.

In Their Own Words

Watch Pastor Mark Vroegop (College Park Church, Carmel, IN) talk about his commitment to "Expositional Preaching" at http://www.64fellowship.com/oldpaths/21/

We have a balance to strike—not
to preach Christ without preaching
the text, and not to preach the text
without preaching Christ.[1]

TIMOTHY KELLER

Thou hast shown me that the glory of
everything that is sanctified to do good is
not seen in itself, but in the source of its
sanctification.

Thus my end in preaching is to know
Christ, and impart his truth;
my principle in preaching is Christ
himself, whom I trust, for in him is
fullness of spirit and strength;
my comfort in preaching
is do all for him.

Then, whether I succeed or fail, naught
matters but thee alone.[2]

A PURITAN PRAYER

10

Men to Match the Message

Twice in my ministry journey, I became the senior pastor of a large church in the wake of a tragic moral failure. Each of my predecessors was a gifted man with extraordinary communication skills. However, when the facts about their long-term lifestyles emerged, it became painfully clear that each man in the pulpit was not the same one who lived within the walls of the home or even the hallways of the church offices.

Let's be honest. Every pastor feels the pull and plight of duplicity to some degree. As Paul declared, "Who is adequate for these things?" (2 Cor. 2:16 NASB). One penitent Puritan writer prayed:

> Oh God, I know that I often do thy work without thy power,
> and sin by my dead, heartless, blind service, my lack of inward
> light, love, delight, my mind, heart, tongue moving without thy
> help. I see sin in my heart in seeking the approbation of others.
> This is my vileness, to make men's opinion my rule, whereas I
> should see what good I have done and give thee glory, consider
> what sin I have committed and mourn for that. It is my deceit
> to preach, and pray, and to stir up others' spiritual affections in
> order to beget commendations, where my rule should be daily to
> consider myself more vile than any man in my own eyes.[3]

We know that a shallow life makes for a conflicted ministry. A compartmentalized pulpit is a dangerous one. While the threefold commitment of understanding, unction, and utterance is vital to the task of preaching, there are other characteristics that every preacher must pursue to enjoy a life of impact and endurance. What do we need to embrace as we return to the old paths of Acts 6:4, especially as we think of an empowered and enduring ministry of the Word of God? At this point character matters, as pastor and author Carey Nieuwhof reminds us:

> Character—far more than skill set—determines how deeply and passionately people follow you. A leader with character is a leader worth following. A leader who lacks integrity may have followers, but he'll never gain their full trust or their hearts. After all, we all know highly skilled leaders who are never truly embraced; they're merely tolerated. Character, more than anything else, draws the hearts of people to your leadership.[4]

The Scriptures are clear on the nature of and need for character among those who lead the church, as outlined in 1 Timothy 3:1–3 and Titus 1:5–9. Nothing I could add would enhance these in any fashion. Yet, consider with me some practical extensions of pastoral character that help shape an environment that might expedite a growing renewal within the church.

WORSHIP-BASED HUMILITY

The key to humility is a high view of God. As Puritan Thomas Watson noted, "A sight of God's glory humbles. The stars vanish when the sun appears."[5]

I've often encouraged my worship team with the reminder that they are not worship leaders but rather lead worshipers. Those of us who preach must also look in the mirror and give the same admonition. As a preacher, I am a lead worshiper. The sermon must be birthed in worship, shaped in worship, and delivered as an act of passionate worship.

When we are captivated by the biblical truth of the worthiness of God, we will be humbled with the undeniable reality of the neediness of our own hearts. Such Godward focus and imbedded self-effacement spreads through the sermon like smoke pouring around the roofline and out the windows of a house on fire.

John Calvin wrote, "So long as we do not look beyond the earth, we are quite pleased with our own righteousness, and wisdom and virtue; we address ourselves in the most flattering tone, and seem only less than demigods."[6] Many in our congregations watch preachers perform week after week, flaunting the latest technology, celebrating program statistics, and featuring the images of the stage singers on mega screens. I've often said, "Pride is like bad breath—everyone knows you have it but you."

The spirit of an awakening is sparked when pastors experience and express a new humility that would shape the environment in their churches. The apostle James calls all followers to yield to the Spirit:

> Or do you suppose it is to no purpose that the Scripture says,
> "He yearns jealously over the spirit that he has made to dwell in
> us"? But he gives more grace. Therefore it says, "God opposes
> the proud, but gives grace to the humble." Submit yourselves
> therefore to God. Resist the devil, and he will flee from you.
> Draw near to God, and he will draw near to you. Cleanse your
> hands, you sinners, and purify your hearts, you double-minded.
> . . . Humble yourselves before the Lord, and he will exalt you.
> (James 4:5–10)

What might this look like as the environment of church next Sunday? Great grace. Victory over the enemy. The nearness of

God. Purity. Superficial happiness replaced by repentance, leading to a true exaltation of the work of the Gospel by God's mighty hand.

Calvin urged a high view of God as core to this humility:

> But should we once begin to raise our thoughts to God, and reflect what kind of Being he is, and how absolute the perfection of that righteousness and wisdom and virtue to which, as a standard, we are bound to be conformed, what formerly delighted us by its false show of righteousness will become polluted with the greatest iniquity; what strangely imposed upon us under the name of wisdom will disgust by its extreme folly; and what presented the appearance of virtuous energy will be condemned as the most miserable impotence.[7]

Humility is not announced by our noble deeds like a hot-air balloon in the Macy's Thanksgiving Day Parade. Rather, humility is perceived in the essence of our life and teaching, much like the aroma of quality cologne. It is organic to our persona in ways that do not have to be described, and usually cannot be articulated.

COMPASSIONATE LOVE

Years ago, musical artist B. J. Thomas recorded a popular song, "Using Things and Loving People," which included the truthful line "Loving things and using people only leads to misery."[8] The danger exists for any preacher to love the pulpit and use the people rather than loving people and using the pulpit. Preaching is one of the great expressions of God's heart of love for His people. Our flesh can sometimes bring us to the point of loving the preaching (the crowd, the impact, the personal fulfillment) and using people for our own significance and satisfaction.

Knowing this temptation over the years, I have prayed as I

approach the pulpit to preach, "Lord, help me to look out on a family to be loved, not a crowd to be feared." We could add, "Not a crowd to be used." I have needed that reminder countless times as it reframes my attitude in the preaching moment.

You and I need to model Paul's ministry among the Thessalonian church: "But we were gentle among you, like a nursing mother taking care of her own children. So, being affectionately desirous of you, we were ready to share with you not only the gospel of God but also our own selves, because you had become very dear to us" (1 Thess. 2:7–8). No more tender and compassionate imagery could capture Paul's love for the Thessalonian church.

Spurgeon lamented, "We have grown professional in our service, and now we preach like automatons, wound up for a sermon, to run down when the discourse is over. And we have little more care for the souls of men than if they were so much dirt."[9]

In the extended description of genuine love in 1 Corinthians 13 it is notable that Paul used the first-person singular in the text. He spoke personally of his gifts, his preaching, his understanding, his faith, and his life of sacrifice. Then the apostle issued the startling conclusion that without love his ministry would just be "a noisy gong or a clanging cymbal." He would be nothing and gain nothing (1 Cor. 13:1–3). This reality must grip the heart of every spiritual leader as we interpret and apply this

Our hearts must be overwhelmed with Christ's heart for the lost, hurting, and broken.

standard to our own attitudes and approaches in ministry, and preaching in particular.

I have defined love as "an act of self-sacrifice, flowing from the heart, produced by the Holy Spirit—for the good of others and the glory of God." This does not mean that our self-sacrifice should lead to self-annihilation and the destruction of our family as we try to meet every need, make every hospital visit, counsel every troubled soul, and attend every committee meeting. The Bible is clear that deacon-type servants and gifted saints can conduct many of those tasks. What it does mean is that the fulfillment of essential ministry priorities (see chap. 4) must be motivated and marked by biblical love. "Let all that you do be done in love" (1 Cor.16:14).

Paul defined the essence of the Christian faith—and accordingly the Christian ministry—as "faith working through love" (Gal. 5:6). This is best understood as faith energized or produced by love.[10] Our calling to defend the faith, preach the faith, and live the faith is all energized by love.

Of course, we are not just preachers, but shepherds, called to care for the sheep entrusted to our oversight. As the Good Shepherd was moved with compassion at the condition of the wandering sheep, so must our hearts be overwhelmed with His heart for the lost, hurting, and broken. We are to lead and preach sacrificially, willingly, and as examples of Christ, the Chief Shepherd (1 Peter 5:1–4).

The old adage still rings true, "People don't care how much you know until they know how much you care." Paul underscores a love-driven pulpit with this overarching declaration, "The aim of our charge is love that issues from a pure heart and a good conscience and a sincere faith."

GODLY AUTHENTICITY

As I was writing this book, I posted a question on Facebook, asking my circle of friends what they thought was the most important quality of a pastor, especially as he preached from the pulpit. Among almost two hundred responses, the top two were humility (addressed above) and authenticity/transparency. I've heard it said many times that people admire our strengths but identify with our weaknesses.

Pastor Carey Nieuwhof frames it this way,

> Being an authentic leader is hardly negotiable anymore. People
> want to see the *real* you, with your weaknesses, mistakes, and
> vulnerabilities. You know that, because you're watching the last
> fumes of the "never let 'em see you sweat" leader vaporize into
> the stratosphere. But you've also seen the pendulum swing the
> other way. You don't want to be the "oversharing" transparent
> person on your Facebook newsfeed whose every emotion, rela-
> tional struggle and moment of self-doubt is posted for the planet
> to gawk at.[11]

Nieuwhof offers three helpful guidelines for managing transparency. First he wisely suggests that a leader process current
issues privately, within a tight-knit circle (i.e., spouse, elders, close
friends, mentors, and counselors). "Just because *somebody* needs
to know about them doesn't mean *everybody* needs to know about
them," Nieuwhof writes. "Discretion and transparency are not a
contradiction at all. Telling the right people is often the difference
between success and failure in ministry."

Next, Nieuwhof counsels a leader to express publicly only what
he's processed privately and to share only what will help the lis-
tener, not himself. Using the pulpit to divulge the struggles and
lessons of a personal journey is never intended to draw attention
to the preacher. The Sunday service is not the context for personal
therapy or a solicitation of affirmation. The goal is to honor Christ
and empower and equip the church with practical applications of
truth, often flowing from the preacher's life.

It is true the apostle Paul disclosed a mysterious visit to the
"third heaven" followed by his honest admission of a "thorn in the
flesh" and his struggle of unanswered prayer. This transparency,
however, led to an exaltation of Christ's grace, best experienced in
abject weakness (2 Cor. 12:1–10). Of course, Paul never disclosed

this experience until writing to the Corinthians many years later, when he knew the story would be helpful and relevant to his teaching goal. This is a good model for transparency in the preaching environment.

Personal genuineness is rooted in a life of worship and prayer. Vulnerability before God brings a security that makes vulnerability before people comfortable. A leader who seeks God's face, personally and with His people, cannot help but desire authenticity. This honest, open, sincere relationship becomes a vital and comfortable part of the fabric of pulpit ministry. We cannot fake the Christian life behind the cloak of preaching.

> *A leader who seeks God's face personally . . . cannot help but desire authenticity.*

Neither should we ever fake the sermon for the sake of an obligatory weekend performance. John MacArthur offers a good reminder:

> Pastoral integrity is crucial. The issue here is not your sermon. God's Word is at stake here. If you have not had time to prepare, then preach something you have had time to prepare. Just tell the folks that next Sunday you will come back to the text you had planned to preach on, that you need more time to work through. There is never any virtue in preaching for the sake of preaching. The only virtue is in proclaiming truth—truth that you cannot preach until you know what it is.[12]

I would add that this includes truth that you cannot preach until you have applied it to your own life and struggles, based on a solid understanding of the text. Pastor Timothy Keller says it well, "The temptation will be to let the pulpit drive you to the Word, but instead you must let the Word drive you to the pulpit. Prepare the preacher more than you prepare the sermon."[13]

In Their Own Words

Watch Pastor Keeney Dickenson (First Baptist Church, Crockett, TX) share about "The Priority of Prayer and Transparency" at http://www.64fellowship.com/oldpaths/22/

RESOLUTE DEPENDENCE

Often, as I speak to pastors' groups, the question is asked, "Where should I start with the prayer emphasis in my church?" I always recommend they begin with a regular time of prayer on Sunday mornings, prior to the worship service. In my case, we met early for twenty years (typically from 6:30 to 7:30 a.m.). This gave our worship team time to get ready for the services and even allowed those who lived in close proximity to the church facility the opportunity to return home to get ready or retrieve the family.

I recommend this beginning point for several reasons:

1. As the pastor, you feel an extraordinary sense of need as you are about to impart the Word and lead people in worship.
2. Few people have major schedule conflicts at this time.
3. It's Sunday, so church is naturally on the mind of many people, which makes it a high-profile opportunity.
4. It serves as a great training environment for those who may eventually lead this kind of prayer experience *during* the worship services, as you are preaching.

It was said of Spurgeon that he was a preacher who was made by the prayers of his people. Sunday intercession creates a direct and cognizant link between the priority of prayer and the impact of the preached Word. Sponsoring this prayer focus and giving it regular emphasis ensures that people recognize the hand of God in the worship and preaching. It is all rooted in the praying—not the talent of the preacher or the skill of the musicians. The preacher models humble reliance on God. Christ gets the glory.

In his *Lectures to My Students*, Spurgeon spoke of a fellow preacher whose ministry was profoundly fruitful but who came to realize that the impact was not due to his talent or eloquence but rather to a man in his church who had labored in intercessory prayer for Spurgeon's preaching. "It may in the all-revealing day be so with us," Spurgeon then comments. "We may discover, after having labored long and wearily in preaching, that all the honor belongs to another builder, whose prayers were gold, silver and precious stones. While our sermonizings being apart from prayer were but hay and stubble."[14] Years later, Spurgeon said, "Truly I wish that all pastors could always, without doubt, assume that they enjoyed the perpetual prayer of those under their charge."[15]

In my decades of preaching, I felt a great need to make this a priority. It required my own early morning example. It meant that I would train people to lead these times of intercession during the services. We gave it visibility virtually every Sunday, noting that we had people in the prayer room, interceding for the impact of the Word and the heart transformation among the listeners. When we did not have substantive prayer support, I tasked a deacon to notify me so that I could appeal for more intercessors before I preached. Spurgeon underscores this priority, "The sinew of the minister's strength under God is the supplication of his church. We can do anything and everything if we have a praying people around us."[16]

Effective preaching must be understood as a supernatural work, not just an intellectual exercise. A resolute, visible dependence on the prayers of God's people elevates the work of the Spirit for the glory of God. Of course, only heaven will reveal the ultimate impact of these prayers, but the services will surely reflect the promised blessing to those who call upon the name of the Lord on behalf of the declaration of the Word of God.

GOSPEL PASSION

A worship-based humility, compassionate love, godly authenticity, and resolute dependence all must lead to a passion for the Christ of the Gospel and the Gospel of Christ. Worship of a holy God by a sinful man always exalts the reconciling grace of the Gospel, because apart from the cross we could never worship "in spirit and truth" (John 4:24). Compassionate love is always rooted in the great truth that we love because He first loved us (1 John 4:19). Our love for our people as we proclaim His truth is only possible because His love is living through us via of the power of the cross. Godly authenticity points to the work of the Gospel in taking a frail and fallen man, and sanctifying him through the trials of life into the image of Christ (Rom. 8:29–30). Resolute dependence points to the immeasurable greatness of His power toward us, revealed in Christ, to the praise of His glory (Eph.1:12, 19).

Paul's understanding of the Holy Spirit's wisdom and power in preaching kept him focused like a laser-guided missile, "For I decided to know nothing among you except Jesus Christ and Him crucified." All our preaching, whether from the Old Testament passage, a New Testament text, or a contemporary topic of interest, must get to Jesus quickly and adorn the message of the Gospel. "Every time you expound a Bible text," Keller concludes, "you are not finished unless you demonstrate how it shows us that we cannot save ourselves and that only Jesus can."[17]

As we pursue the old paths of preaching ministry, we will be compelled to preach "all the words of this life" (Acts 5:20). This is the hope of proclaiming the truth of the Gospel with humility, love, authenticity, and dependence on the Spirit's graces through the prayers of His people. With this resolve, we can serve in the promised reality of new power and the glorious experience of His manifest presence in our midst.

In Their Own Words

Watch revival leader Richard Owen Roberts talk about "The Word as Hammer, Fire and Sword" at http://www.64fellowship.com/oldpaths/23/

The essence of true religion is spontaneity, the sovereign moving of the Holy Spirit upon and in the free spirit of redeemed men. This has through the years of human history been the hallmark of spiritual excellence, the evidence of reality in a word of unreality.[1]

A. W. TOZER

Each week Christians contend with the pressures of strained budgets, stressful jobs, sickly bodies, and fragile relationships. Consequently, more is needed on the Lord's Day than mere enthusiasm from a motivational speaker. More is needed than a fresh set of techniques from the latest pop-psychologist. It is the voice of the living Christ that people need to hear through the preaching of the evangelical scripture: to sense the power and efficacy of the Spirit most sensibly accompanying the word.[2]

ARTURO G. ARZUDIA III

11

"God Is Truly Among You"

The Barna Group recently reported that 46 percent of church attenders testified that "their life had not changed at all as a result of churchgoing." Asked to think about their last church visit, three out of five (61 percent) said they could not remember a significant or important new insight or understanding related to faith. Even among those who attended church *in the past week,* half admitted they could not recall a significant insight they had gained. Beyond this, one-third of those who had attended a church in the past had never felt God's presence while in a congregational setting.[3]

In contrast, when a leader has embraced the old paths declared in Acts 6:4—the paths of "prayer and the ministry of the word"—as the primary task of ministry, a new culture in the church emerges. This freshness is ultimately evidenced in the worship gatherings of the congregation. Lives do change. In an environment of prayer and Spirit-empowered preaching, with fresh applications of truth, something inexplicably supernatural occurs in the hearts of attenders.

Ironically, when leaders sense a lack of vibrancy in their weekend gatherings they may dismiss the old paths and turn to new techniques for attracting more people and appealing to a younger crowd. In doing so, they risk not only subjugating the power of the Holy Spirit, but reducing the worship experience to a presentation that fails in many ways to accomplish the goal.

Barna Research frames this well, especially in our attempts to reach a new generation:

> It's tempting to think of church as one part of the "religious services industry"—the sector of the economy that provides spiritual goods and experiences to consumers. When leaders conceive of their faith community this way, even unconsciously, they see their difficulty appealing to Millennials as a failure to create brand loyalty—a failure whose solution is a better product and/ or better marketing. To be successful in the industry, churches have to compete in a marketplace undergoing massive disruption as a generation of young consumers becomes ever more knowledgeable and selective about what they do and don't want.
>
> If the church were just another business seeking market share, this frame of mind would be harmless or even beneficial. But the church is not. And many of the very people churches are trying to reach—Millennials—are hyperaware and deeply suspicious of the intersection of church and consumer culture. This doesn't mean they're not avid consumers, for most certainly are. But many also have a sense that church should be different somehow, above or beyond the dirty business of *sell, sell, sell*.[4]

Among those in this generation who say church is not important, most are split between two reasons: two in five say church is not important because they can find God elsewhere (39 percent), and one-third say it's because church is not personally relevant to them (35 percent).[5]

These realities should compel us to a new awareness that the antithesis of "sell" and "attract" are "substance and awe." If the young generation does not believe that church is the one place to truly encounter the living Christ in the most relevant and life-changing experience known on earth, then we must ask, "What are we doing?" What is the purpose of our weekend gatherings after all? Is our current approach accomplishing Christ's design for His people? Is the substance of our worship gatherings leaving people in awe of a living Christ or just impressed (maybe suspicious, as Barna says) with our efforts to gain more market share?

GOD SENT HIS SON
FOR . . . A TARGET AUDIENCE?

In many churches the goal has been to focus on a target audience. Everything in the weekend services and the design of other programming is intended to attract and hold a particular demographic, often at the exclusion of anyone outside that bull's-eye. This thinking is the fruit of the church growth movement and current gurus who declare that the primary goal of Sunday services is to attract a crowd of entertained and comfortable prospects.

Of course, this is contrary to the essence of the Gospel. God did not send His Son for a target audience but for a lost world. In addition, the whole illustration of the congregation as a physical body described in First Corinthians 12 argues for diversity and multiplicity in the local assembly, which would include variances in age, race, and social status. No target audience (body part) should be valued and overemphasized above another.

Yet we may rely on studies, borrowed strategies, and formulaic programs to attract a specific slice of the community pie. Sadly, all the superficial research and designated techniques that must be used to "target" our message can soon become a cheap replacement for the ultimately relevant and cross-generational power of the work of the Spirit.

THE MEASUREMENT THAT MATTERS

Often all of our investigation, targeting, devising, and enticements are rooted in the wrong measurements for a church. In my observation, when pastors get together to talk about their churches, 90 percent of the conversation centers around attendance, budget, and buildings. We love these "measurables." Certainly, every soul matters, and resources are necessary to reach our world for Christ. But most often, Sunday statistics and square footage capacities are a way for pastors to find their place in the ecclesiastical pecking order—leading to either a sense of superiority or inferiority; elation or depression.

By the way, I get it. I have been a church planter with very little quantifiable braggadocio and I have shepherded thousands while paying on a 350,000 square foot facility. I have felt the inferiority and prideful validation on both ends, and everything in between. But it all matters little in the final analysis.

News flash! When we stand before Christ there will be no mention of attendance, budget, and buildings. Remember Paul's words:

> For no one can lay a foundation other than that which is laid, which is Jesus Christ. Now if anyone builds on the foundation with gold, silver, precious stones, wood, hay, straw—each one's work will become manifest, for the Day will disclose it, because it will be revealed by fire, and the fire will test what sort of work each one has done. If the work that anyone has built on the foundation survives, he will receive a reward. If anyone's work is burned up, he will suffer loss, though he himself will be saved, but only as through fire. (1 Cor. 3:11–15)

The final accounting of our ministry will not be the "size" of ministry we forged but the "sort" of ministry we shaped. This final assessment will not be based merely on what we did, but why we did it, how we did it, and for whom.

The final accounting of our ministry will not be based on merely what we did, but why we did it, how we did it, and for whom.

Paul tells us what every spiritual leader's goal should be when Jesus returns: "For what is our hope or joy or crown of boasting before our Lord Jesus at his coming? Is it not you? For you are our glory and joy" (1 Thess. 2:19–20). We know nothing about the attendance figures or budget for the church in Thessalonica. Paul trumpeted their love, their faith, their joy—their spiritual character.

The quality of the lives of the people who have been influenced by our ministry will be the acid test of eternity. Paul notes that the faithfulness and fruitfulness of his followers will be the final assessment of a life of reward vs. vain pursuit (Phil. 2:16). He understood that the character of his disciples would be his only boast before Christ and his "joy and his crown" in eternity (2 Cor. 1:14; Phil. 4:1).

Paul's words offer a riveting reality check for us all as we pray, preach, and plan our services. "Therefore do not pronounce judgment before the time, before the Lord comes, who will bring to light the things now hidden in darkness and will disclose the purposes of the heart. Then each one will receive his commendation from God" (1 Cor. 4:5).

TARGET A TRANSFORMATIONAL EXPERIENCE!

With this in mind, we should leave a target audience and seek a target experience—one that is transformational, week after week, and that produces a certain kind of Christ follower. When we seek

OLD PATHS, NEW POWER

a transformational experience, it is powerfully relevant to any and every audience. A true New Testament experience transcends age, race, status, and even spiritual conditions—lost or saved.

Since there is only one mention in the New Testament that describes the presence of a non-believer encountering a Christian worship gathering, we are wise to explore the exact goal of that moment. Paul describes it this way: "But if all prophesy, and an unbeliever or outsider enters, he is convicted by all, he is called to account by all, the secrets of his heart are disclosed, and so, falling on his face, he will worship God and declare that God is really among you" (1 Cor. 14:24–25).

According to this text, the target experience is rooted in the power of "prophecy" (preaching) that brings conviction. The manifestation of the power of truth is seen in the people and sensed among the people. A holy accountability to the truth of the Gospel grips the exposed heart. With a consciousness of penetrating conviction the participant is moved to Gospel-propelled and self-abandoned worship. His commentary on it all is "God is truly among you."

The goal is not to be impressed with the targeting techniques, the media capabilities, the facility, or even the friendliness of the people. Instead, the "visitor" is to be in awe of the living Christ who is undeniably powerful and present in the lives of His people. This is the reality of the glory of God—the magnification of the person of Christ by His people and the manifestation of the presence of Christ within His people.

Maybe that's why Jim Cymbala declared at a one-day pastors' event, "Our great fear should not be that people leave our church but that they would stay in our church and remain unchanged." In a similar vein, Cymbala has written, "Nowhere in the Bible do we see example of Christ followers watering down or holding back parts of the message in order to hold the crowd. They preached the

Gospel with power and let God take care of the numbers."[6]

I believe when pastors return to the priority and sufficiency of "prayer and the ministry of the word" as the supernatural essence of their ministry function, spiritual passion will naturally overflow in the dynamics of what happens in every facet of the church, especially the weekend worship service. A new sense of the sufficiency of the Holy Spirit will shape the planning, the praying, the preaching, and the product of the gathering of God's people.

As was noted in a previous chapter, it is best to build the sidewalks where the footpaths already exist. The most important environment in church life where a prayer culture flourishes is in the context of the weekend worship experience.

Yet our service planning seldom includes or anticipates any significant experiences of prayer. Our tech sheet is planned to the final second with songs, announcements, offerings, video clips, special music, and a sermon that is regulated by the countdown clock more than by the promptings of the Holy Spirit. At best, prayer is modeled as a perfunctory open and close, and includes sincere petitions for the people's health needs.

In Their Own Words

Watch Pastor Jim Cymbala (The Brooklyn Tabernacle, Brooklyn, NY) share an amazing story about "Obeying Holy Spirit Promptings" as told at The 6:4 Fellowship National Conference at http://www.64fellowship.com/oldpaths/24/

WORSHIP INTERRUPTED

While pastoring in Minnesota, we decided to regularly leave at least five minutes of unallocated time in the worship services. With more than four thousand people in multiple services, a packed children's ministry, and a crowded parking lot, we needed to try to stick to the designated time frames. But within the available seventy-five-minute service allotment, we left room for the Holy Spirit to prompt a moment of prayer. Sometimes it would happen before the sermon, during the sermon, at the end of the sermon, or mid-stream during the musical worship.

On one occasion, we were singing a newer song about the majesty of Christ. I sensed a need to bring greater application of that amazing theme—and had the freedom to do it.

At the Spirit's prompting, I came to the microphone and signaled my worship pastor that I would like to interrupt. I began to ask the congregation a series of questions:

"What would we do if the president of the United States and his entourage of bodyguards and assistants walked into the worship center right now? How would we respond?

"More importantly, what would we do if the resurrected Christ suddenly appeared before our physical eyes, as He did for John in Revelation chapter one? Would it be just another Sunday of perfunctory worship?

"What will we do when we stand in His holy presence in the company of all the saints and angels of heaven? We are in His presence. He is here in our midst. So whatever we think we will do on that day—let us do it right now."

The people understood the questions and the instruction. While I did not suggest any particular response, it was clear that the Spirit was letting everyone know what He had in mind. It was a remarkable sight. Young and old alike reacted with immediate sensitivity but profound diversity. Some stood in rapt attention, staring to the sky as if looking at the Savior's face. Others sat, face in hands, projecting a humble heart. Some maneuvered between the theater-style seats and knelt in reverence. Many stood with hands upstretched in passionate praise. The aisles filled with people stepping outside the seating area to find a place to bow. I was told that many lay prostrate on the carpet in abandonment before His holy presence.

Personally, I witnessed none of this. Others described the response to me later. I had already walked to

The aisles filled with people stepping outside the seating area to find a place to bow.

a quiet corner of the stage and was facedown in His presence. I understand the worship team on the platform reflected similar freedom as those in the pews. Tears flowing, our worship pastor fell to his knees to lead the congregation in a few mores choruses of the song, followed by passionate prayers of confession and worship.[7]

It was a holy moment. A timeless moment. I was grateful we had the freedom to deviate from the carefully planned tech sheet. We could not afford to miss moments like this. That day will forever be etched in our minds as an occasion when we got beyond the formula of the service to encounter Christ in the service. God was "truly among us" as we left room for Him to bring application to our hearts.

RETHINKING THE TRADITION

Have you ever asked why we plan our services the way we do? They are incredibly predictable with planned segments of music, announcements, offering, and a sermon. What if we integrated these elements in a fresh and cohesive way—blending multiple, shorter segments of teaching with prayerful response and thematically related singing? (See Appendix 5 for some even more radical ideas about what we might do to better facilitate a sense of the centrality and presence of Christ, and the value of the body, in our services.[8])

A fresh experience of Christ in our worship services is possible and needed, writes Cymbala:

OLD PATHS, NEW POWER

Sadly, I have learned that even many church leaders themselves have never experienced the awesomeness of God's presence. All they know about is how to "do church." They are basically technicians who know how to keep it "moving," upbeat, funny and technically impressive with excellence in music. The worship of God is thus reduced to little more than a well-rehearsed production. The time for openness to the Spirit, free-flowing praise or prayer—this is anathema to contemporary church philosophy. To have unscripted time in which the Holy Spirit might manifest himself so that people could actually experience God himself rather than just facts about him is unthinkable! That would take the control out of our hands, and the well-rehearsed production would be ruined. No wonder so many are leaving the church and Christianity is declining. We don't seem to want God to visit us. We would rather have the human than the Divine.[9]

A. W. Tozer notes how this constrains the work of the Holy Spirit in our churches:

> Because the Holy Spirit is not given a chance to work in our service, nobody is repenting, nobody is seeking God, nobody is spending a day in quiet waiting on God with open Bible seeking to mend his or her ways. . . . For the most part, spiritual rigidity that cannot bend is too weak to know just how weak it is.[10]

May God make us bold. Let us ask Him to make us sensitive and flexible, and to keep our motives pure. May we be ready for something fresh and supernatural for the sake of the Gospel.

In Their Own Words

Watch Francis Chan share his heart on "The Role of Holy Spirit in Preaching" at http://www.64fellowship.com/oldpaths/25/

ON THE PATH TO POWER

The Acts 6:4 Balance
ALISTAIR BEGG

In the midst of the many demands of pastoral ministry, certain commitments must be maintained to keep the priority of the "ministry of the word."

There has to be, first of all, a conviction about the place of the Word of God—its sufficiency and its authority. And until a man really has that, everything will be fairly superficial. Once he's absolutely convinced that it is the Word of God that does the work of God, then he simply becomes an agent in that process.

One of the great safeguards is to do systematic and consecutive ministry. So your congregation knows that you're supposed to be at verse 7 next week because you were at verse 6 last week. This serves as a positive reminder for keeping one's nose to the grindstone and being prepared to sit there and labor in the text. It is one of the disciplines a pastor puts in place so that the study of the Word of God has priority, not only in the way he frames his time, but also in the way he thinks.

When I reflect on the disciplines I have put in place to help in my preaching, I recognize maybe next week will be the right week in terms of the impact of the sermon. I don't think that I have really mastered peculiar skills in relationship to those things. It is the sufficiency of the Bible that I must depend on.

In Scotland it was much easier for me, ironically, when I was all by myself. The mornings were for study, the afternoons were for visitation, and the evenings were for the meetings. And if I didn't set it out that way and establish those disciplines, then things would crumble on me pretty quickly. Now, I have a pastoral team with multiple people and all that comes with it. People say, "Oh, that's terrific." I used to think that when I got to this point, things would be so much easier. In actual fact, I don't find it easier. I find that the demands that are placed upon one in relationship to the team and the expectations of people make it even harder to fight against distraction.

Now, I actually have disciplines in relationship to the geography of our buildings. I have a study that's in the flow of the offices, but then I have another place I call "The Cave." I go to The Cave to study and the people around the building say: "He's probably in The Cave." They know when I'm in The Cave I need to stay there for as long as I have to stay there because "Sunday cometh."

I also have mechanisms in the actual approach to Bible study. These are the descriptors that I took from the old boys in Scotland a long time ago. I start by "thinking myself empty." I come to the passages, pray over them, read them, and then scribble down anything that comes to mind, whatever it is. I don't even worry about it, even if it's silly stuff, I put it all down.

Then I proceed to "reading myself full." That is not simply reading commentaries, but having the opportunity to read other related material, depending on time. From there, I go to "writing myself clear." That writing process for me is absolutely crucial and I think it's a neglected process in a number of pastors' lives. They wind up doing the hard work while they are preaching. They are bringing their congregation into the process with them, rather than having done the hard work on their own.

Writing myself clear has been a huge discipline to me. I guess I got it from Spurgeon who said: "Write out your sermons in full for the first five years." I did that for the first five years, and then I never found any reason to stop. Think myself empty, read myself full, write myself clear. Finally, I seek to "pray myself hot." Once in the pulpit, I also learned that I need to be myself and forget myself.

In relation to the priorities of "prayer and the ministry of the word" a man may have a greater commitment to prayer and a lesser commitment to the Word. Conversely, he may have a great passion for the Word of God and little concern for prayer. I think the latter is far more dangerous than the former, and I think that latter is probably where most of us are more guilty. We move too quickly to the processes of study, thinking that perhaps we can catch up with the prayer, or we will deal with the prayer later on, or we'll pray as we go or whatever else it is. And the devil, of course, is masterful at explaining to us why we should do that. I'm not so sure that there is much of a danger in the former, because I myself have never got that balance wrong on that end.

My father used to tell me that for every five minutes you preach, you should be praying three times as much: a quarter hour of prayer for every five minutes of delivery. So if you preach for forty minutes you have prayed for two hours. Thus the delivery is saturated in prayer.

It's seldom that I can honestly say that I get there, and I think the danger is far more in thinking that I'm going to do better if I spend longer in preparation for my talking, than I will do if I'm actually praying. I think the same is true in other areas as well. We tend to think that as long as we are talking to somebody about the Lord, that's where it's truly happening. But in actual fact, we can do more than pray *after* we prayed, but we can't do more than pray *until* we have prayed.

When we fail to strike the proper balance of "prayer and the ministry of the word" it results in dryness, formalism, and ultimately spiritual sterility. I think it was E. M. Bounds who said, "The devil laughs at prayerless preaching." The enemy understands the spiritual dynamic that is involved in God choosing to take someone and use him. This prayerless preaching is a particular danger to a man who has a pretty good gift. When someone seems to have an "inferior gift," if we can refer to it in that way, he knows himself to be inept and can only cry to God before, during, and after. Ironically, when we begin to have any measure of facility, particularly with language, we can begin to think that our verbal effectiveness is synonymous with spiritual impact. In much the same way that we tend to think that giftedness is the issue; but in fact, godliness is the issue. You can be gifted without being godly and you can be a very able speaker but really not be doing very much at all except tickling people's ears and impressing them. The spiritual work that actually takes place when God's Word is really taught and God's voice is really heard comes from seeking God, crying out to Him for spiritual empowerment.

Proud people don't pray because they don't believe they need to. The worst thing that can happen is for a man to be regarded as being really useful when actually he's not. People might say his ministry is one of gold, silver, and precious stones. God may say it is wood, hay, and stubble. And the tragedy would be that the man wouldn't find out until he arrived at the finishing line.

Adapted from an interview with The 6:4 Fellowship—www.64 fellowship.com. Used by permission.

AN OLD PATHS PROFILE
PASTOR JEFF WELLS

JEFF WELLS is pastor at Woods Edge Community Church in a northwest suburb of Houston. Jeff was a four-time All-American recipient in track and cross country while at Rice University. Today, he has converted that passion into a run for the prize of the high calling of Christ to be a man of "prayer and the ministry of the word"—and to lead a praying church.

Prayer has been the engine of this fruitful ministry, both at WoodsEdge Community and multiple planted churches. Even though Wells has advanced degrees from Dallas Theological Seminary, he has resolved to embed pervasive prayer into the church as a vital corollary to his strong biblical teaching.

Wells unashamedly declares the weekly Wednesday Prayer Service as the most important service of the week. The church website states, "We want a prayer service full of expectant people, passionate worship, powerful intercession, regular miracles and an unexplainable sense of God's presence." Concurrent with the prayer meeting, full programming is provided for children and youth.

Every Wednesday from 6:30 to 7:00 p.m. the church auditorium is open for individual prayer. Trained prayer partners, staff, and elders are available to provide personal intercession for those who come. Then, from 7:00 to 8:15 p.m., Wells leads a worship-based prayer service. Wells testifies, "I have a dream—and this dream is my daily prayer—that we would pack out our prayer service. The reason I want this is because I believe that God would honor it. If that many people showed up with a fervent heart to seek the Lord and to pray together and cry out to God, I believe we would see more breakthroughs for the kingdom. More breakthroughs in our personal lives, our families, our community, and in our city. That we would more likely to see our overall vision be realized, that Houston would become a city of God. My dream is that the presence of God and the passion for God would be so strong in the prayer service that people could not stay away."

The church website includes a special video message, allowing Pastor Jeff to share his passion clearly for all those interested in the essence of WoodsEdge. The church boldly promotes prayer; staff time, budgeting, and facilities reflect this priority. The church has a dedicated 24/7 prayer room at the campus. To emphasize this round-the-clock prayer effort, church leaders encourage members to sign up for thirty-minute prayer slots.

Other regular prayer opportunities include a prayer chain, specialized prayer gatherings for key ministry groups in the church, a community prayer walk, an intercessors' prayer chain, and participation in a monthly community-wide "One Heart" prayer gathering on the first Thursday morning of the month.

The WoodsEdge dream for the prayer ministry is described in these words: "We desire to become a church where prayer is seen as the real work. We desire to be known as a House of Prayer that people throughout the community come to for prayer when they have special needs. We desire to become a church family who sees themselves as intercessors, who are quick to pray for others."

All of this effort flows from the heart of the senior pastor. As Pastor Jeff says it, "The church will value what the senior pastor values. The prayer service will never thrive unless the senior pastor champions it."

Commenting on our current evangelical environment, Wells laments, "The early church in the book of Acts was clearly devoted to prayer, focused on prayer, yet most of the American church today does not have this same sense of priority and urgency for prayer. No wonder we do not experience the same power of God poured out on our ministries. No wonder we are having so little impact on our culture and our country. Until we recognize how desperate we are for God, and therefore become desperate in prayer—fervent, humble, united prayer—we won't see transformation or breakthroughs like the early church did."

Then, reflecting on his running days, Wells reminds pastors, "We must be willing to start small, invite others, and persevere over the long haul. It's a marathon, not a sprint."

PART 4

FAITHFUL LEADERS AND THE HOPE OF AN AWAKENING FROM GOD

Christianity in the Book of Acts
is not unusual Christianity—it is
normal, usual, typical Christianity
as it was designed to be.[1]

RAY STEDMAN

Rather than missionary disciples of
Christ going into the world, we have a
group of people content to go in circles.[2]

THOM S. RAINER

12

A New Unleashing of Missional Agents

O nce I joined a gathering of faithful believers in Titusville, Florida, for a luncheon and then spoke to them about their role in encouraging their pastors toward a work of revival. While more than forty pastors and ministry leaders met weekly for prayer, these church members would assemble at a second location to pray for the pastors.

Based on the story of Acts 6:1–7, I reminded these intercessors that "prayer and the ministry of the word" are the foremost priorities of their pastoral leaders. But I focused my presentation on the potential each of *them* brought to a future and powerful work of Christ in their community and beyond. We looked at Acts 6:3 (NKJV), "Therefore, brethren, seek out from among you seven men of good reputation, full of the Holy Spirit and wisdom, whom we may appoint over this business." Many commentators believe this was the beginning of a deacon-type ministry. However you label it, God used these seven in profound ways. As we met, I wondered how the Lord might use these faithful Florida believers in similar ways to advance the mission of Christ. Clearly God wants His people to be missional agents.

PASTORAL SUCCESS

My friend Leith Anderson, pastor for over three decades at Wood-dale Church in Eden Prairie, Minnesota, believes churches do more to help pastors succeed than pastors do to help churches succeed. This seems counterintuitive, as we tend to place such great emphasis on the leadership role of a senior pastor. Yet we also know that some problem churches have a voracious appetite for devouring any pastor foolish enough to accept the call. On the other hand, we know that other churches have a long history of spiritual health, unity, and Gospel advancement. No doubt, life-giving congregational environments are the result of both godly guidance and gracious people working together for God's glory.

In Acts 6, we see an extraordinary environment of spiritual health, profound trust, and ministry empowerment. In the face of debilitating division, this was a moment when those in the Je-rusalem church rose to the occasion to help the apostles succeed and, accordingly, the Gospel to advance. While in this book we have focused on the practical application of the apostles' priorities and practices of "prayer and the ministry of the word," we must also assess the vital role of the people and their seven key represen-tatives in the Acts 6 story. In this scene we see an "unleashing of missional agents" who play a necessary and complementary role in supporting the apostles and serving the people. This, too, was an essential part of the expansion of the Gospel and this important revival moment.

An Empowering Environment

Amazingly, these seven men were selected without a nomi-nating committee, a résumé review team, a bylaw enforcement champion, or campaigning of any kind. The apostles actually had confidence in the work of the Spirit, in the hearts of thousands of newer believers, to identify seven specific servants who would take the ministry to a new level of effectiveness.

Could it be that our confidence in the tangible direction of the Holy Spirit has been eclipsed by our emphasis on human leadership strategies? Have we sidelined the Spirit's primacy through extrabiblical procedures? Have we even distrusted His power because of the insecurity ministers feel because they must control virtually every process in the church? It seems we need a new supernatural infusion of trust—both in the Spirit and in the people He calls to serve.

As mentioned earlier, two of my ministry assignments involved serving a senior pastor role at megachurches on the heels of a dreadful moral failure by each of my predecessors. In each case, trust was a low as low as a California lake in the fifth year of a statewide drought. Both times, I was compelled to lead the staff and congregation in extraordinary rhythms of united prayer. A benefit I did not anticipate or script was the restoration of trust. This is because what a person is on their knees—a person is. When leaders pray openly and honestly with their people in pursuit of the face of God, hearts are united with Spirit-imparted affection and understanding. Health overflows.

When leaders pray honestly with their people in pursuit of the face of God, hearts are united with Spirit-imparted affection.

Of course, not all the people participated in these prayer experiences and, for the most part, they remained trapped in hurt and negativity. But for those who engaged in prayer, trust returned to life like daffodils in springtime. The trust sparked a new openness to the work of the Spirit and Christ's calling on our lives. Most churches I encounter could use a fresh infusion of the kind of trust we see in Acts 6:1–7.

It has been said that bylaws, constitutions, committees, voting, and Robert's Rules of Order have one thing in common. They are not in the Bible. I can't help but wonder if they have become artificial replacements for the real work of united prayer and practical reliance on the leadership and guidance of the Holy Spirit. We are always looking for shortcuts and man-made systems to make things "simpler." Yes, extraordinary prayer is not easy, but it is still effective and sufficient. The simpler path of human structures does not always result in spiritual health. To the contrary, they can often divide, confuse, and frustrate.

Fasting to Find the Mind of the Spirit

At this point, let me insert a note about fasting. I have enjoyed personal fasting many times as a vital discipline to enhance my walk with Christ. I have also enjoyed extended fasts in partnership with a friend or in the context of my churches. The Old Testament features a variety of both required and freewill, corporate and individual fasts. Jesus assumed His disciples would fast after His ascension (Matt. 9:15). Yet there are only two instances of corporate fasting in the New Testament. Both are connected to the selection and appointment of leaders.

The first is found in Acts 13:1–3 as the early church launches the Gospel into Asia:

> Now there were in the church at Antioch prophets and teachers, Barnabas, Simeon who was called Niger, Lucius of Cyrene, Manaen a lifelong friend of Herod the tetrarch, and Saul. While they were worshiping the Lord and fasting, the Holy Spirit said, "Set apart for me Barnabas and Saul for the work to which I have called them." Then after fasting and praying they laid their hands on them and sent them off.

The second is recorded in Acts 14:23 and describes the ministry of Paul and Barnabas during their first missionary journey as they were planting churches, encouraging the saints, and selecting leaders (specifically elders). "And when they had appointed elders for them in every church, with prayer and fasting they committed them to the Lord in whom they had believed."

Although fasting is not mentioned in Acts 6 with the selection of the seven, one pattern we clearly see is that leaders are selected and appointed in an environment of prayer (and even fasting), through a pursuit of God's heart and mind, waiting for the direction and confirmation of Holy Spirit.

It's been said that the best time to get rid of a bad leader is before you choose them. Sadly, today we tend to select pastors, elders, deacons, and others to serve in other vital roles based on superficial human indicators. We fixate on talent, education, status, and even past achievements. We utilize nominating committees, references, and voting to make our final decisions about who should serve. While there is nothing inherently wrong with these tools, we are mistaken to neglect extraordinary prayer, and we can be misguided to make these imperative decisions without a united pursuit of the mind and confirmation of the Holy Spirit through fasting. I can't help but wonder if this is at the core of why so many churches are dysfunctional, divided, and directionless. Did we miss the Holy Spirit's plan for the selection of His choices to serve in vital ministry roles?

The board of directors of The 6:4 Fellowship, composed of pastors and business leaders, has often talked about a "6:3 Fellowship" to coincide with The 6:4 Fellowship. This is the dream of godly believers rising up to take on significant ministry and provide much-needed relief and sharper focus for pastors. Any pastor would be ecstatic to have an army of "6:3" missional agents.

Let's look again at the account from Acts 6:3–5 to see how they ease the load of their leaders:

> "Therefore, brothers, pick out from among you seven men of
> good repute, full of the Spirit and of wisdom, whom we will
> appoint to this duty. But we will devote ourselves to prayer and
> to the ministry of the word." And what they said pleased the
> whole gathering, and they chose Stephen, a man full of faith and
> of the Holy Spirit, and Philip, and Prochorus, and Nicanor, and
> Timon, and Parmenas, and Nicolaus, a proselyte of Antioch.

Men like Stephen and Philip appeared on this list. Acts tells us their stories of powerful preaching, evangelism, and even martyrdom. The other five appointees are never again mentioned, but we know God used their lives for His glory in ways that only eternity will reveal.

TWO SPIRIT-EMPOWERED SERVANTS

Martyrdom Leading to a Movement

Stephen was the first named member of this "6:3 Fellowship" of selected servants. We have an account of the acts of the Holy Spirit in and through his life. The impact of Stephen's selection was significant for several reasons.

1. Stephen became the first non-apostle to defend the faith before the Sanhedrin (Acts 6:12).
2. Stephen was the first Christ-follower to be martyred for the faith (Acts 7:57–60).
3. Stephen's martyrdom sparked a great persecution of the church "on that day," which was followed by a scattering of the church of Jerusalem. God used this dispersion to spread the Gospel to Judea, Samaria, and the uttermost parts of the earth.
4. Many believe that Stephen's martyrdom, and especially the dying grace he demonstrated as he fixed his eyes on the

risen Christ and forgave his persecutors (Acts 7:56–60), weighed heavily on Saul's conscience. Saul "approved of his execution" (8:1). Saul's initial response was fierce, increased indignation, but His subsequent encounter with the living Christ led to his conversion and call as an apostle.

Evangelism Leading to Expansion

Philip's life in the Spirit is also notable. He became known as "the evangelist" (Acts 21:8) for obvious reasons.

As persecution scattered the Jerusalem Christians, Philip went to a city of Samaria and served as an agent of the preaching and power of Christ so effectively that a great number turned to Jesus. The result was that "there was much joy in that city" (Acts 8:4–8). In the midst of this Gospel explosion, God led Philip to leave Samaria and go down to an obscure, deserted place in the southern part of the country. Philip was obedient to this counterintuitive prompting and soon encountered just one individual to whom he preached the Gospel. This man was an important Ethiopian court official on his way from Jerusalem back to Africa and, providentially, was already reading Isaiah 53 when Philip encountered him. Philip pointed him to Christ as the fulfillment of the Old Testament. The Ethiopian believed, was baptized, "and went on his way rejoicing" (Acts 8:25–39).

Acts then says, "But Philip was found at Azotus. And passing through, he preached in all the cities till he came to Caesarea"(v. 40 NKJV). Clearly, he was passionate about preaching Christ as a lifestyle wherever he journeyed. Philip then settled in Caesarea. Many commentators believe Phillip likely served Paul when the apostle passed through on a missionary journey and when he was later in custody for two years (23:31–35; 24:23, 27). So what is the significance of this brief character study?

1. Philip was the first one in Acts to preach the Gospel to Gentiles in obedience to Christ's commission, demonstrating the power of Christ to transcend Jewish nationalism and transform non-Jews through the Gospel.

2. Through Philip's explanation and the power of the Spirit, an Ethiopian official became a Christian. His conversion would lead to the spread of the Gospel into Africa.

3. Philip's distinguished reputation as an evangelist inspires every believer to proclaim Christ.

4. Philip also left a legacy of faith through his four unmarried daughters who followed his example of preaching the Gospel (Acts 21:8). As we say, the apples did not fall far from the tree.

THOSE IN OUR PEWS

Here is the point: Who knows if there is a "Stephen" or a "Philip" sitting in the pews of your services this Sunday? Answer: The Holy Spirit knows. This compels us to create an environment of empowerment. Next time there is a need for a solution to an operational challenge or the launching of a new ministry, we should remember Stephen. When we feel a burden for the expansion of the Gospel through the outreach of our church, we should trust the Holy Spirit to raise up a "Philip." Perhaps we would be compelled to call the church to extraordinary prayer. Even a congregational fast would facilitate a fresh discovery of the Spirit's sufficiency and fruitful plans through His choice of new missional agents.

In Their Own Words

Watch Pastor Maurice Hollingsworth (Shelbyville First Baptist Church, Shelbyville, KY) share about "The Role of Prayer in Evangelism" at http://www.64fellowship.com/oldpaths/26/

Recently the leaders at a large, growing church in Colorado were having a real crisis in recruiting workers for the children's ministry. They had tried pulpit announcements, videos, mailings, and personal urging. Finally, they realized the great need was to call on the "Lord of the Harvest" to stir hearts. One weekend, they shared the need in worship services, and then prompted the people to gather in groups of three or four and simply ask the Holy Spirit to stir hearts. This was not a typical experience in the services, so the leaders were not sure how the people would respond. That week more than two hundred people volunteered to serve, simply because of the stirring of hearts that occurred through prayer. God did in just a few minutes what the best human recruitment efforts could not accomplish over many months.

LOOKING FOR MISSIONAL AGENTS

At the Titusville luncheon, I challenged these folks to be Acts 6:3 spiritual champions and to trust God for amazing results. In summary, my challenge focused on seven commitments for all spiritual agents. These could serve as vital prayer targets for pastors as they survey the sea of faces on a Sunday morning. These could also serve as a standard for every believer in the body of Christ.

1. A Heartfelt Commitment to Exemplary Living

The first description of these seven was that they were "of good reputation." Proverbs 22:1 says, "Choose a good reputation over great riches; being held in high esteem is better than silver or gold" (NLT). Paul would later standardize an exemplary reputation as a qualification for church leadership (1 Tim. 3:7). Shakespeare wrote, "The purest treasure mortal time affords is a spotless reputation."[3]

Something obvious caused these seven men to stand out among

the thousands of believers in the early church at this time. Maybe they had a reputation for honesty, hard work, loving others, caring for their family, or sharing Christ with the lost. In any case, their testimony was recognized and notable at this moment in the life of the church. Every pastor should pray and preach with a goal of reputable living and credible witness.

2. A Humble Submission to the Holy Spirit

These seven were also "full of the Holy Spirit." Their character was marked by an extraordinary submission to the Holy Spirit. Accordingly, their elevation to a greater realm of service brought a significant advancement of the mission in the church. Clearly, all seven men were notably dominated by the Spirit and bore the fruit of His power in their lives. We cannot afford the perception that the Holy Spirit is the "Forgotten God," as Francis Chan has titled Him in his popular book.[4] We are compelled to explain biblically, encourage practically, and expect wholeheartedly the sufficiency of the Spirit at work in the hearts of our people.

3. A Hunger for Godly Wisdom

These servants also exemplified lives full of "wisdom." Wisdom is the power of truth applied to the practice of life. Their proven biblical insight, judicious decision-making, and prudent choices brought needed insight and welfare to the present predicament.

4. A Humane Understanding of the Needs

Each of these seven men had Greek names, indicating they were Jews with Greek background and language. This reflected the wisdom of finding men who could effectively relate to the disgruntled Hellenistic widows. This was also a major step toward the cultural diversity that reflected obedience to Jesus' mandate to preach to the nations (Acts 1:8; 11:19–20). There existed then, and is now, considerable value in assigning people to tasks for which they have a natural understanding and genuine concern.

5. A Healthy View of Their Spiritual Potential

Too often, Christians today view themselves as mere "laymen." I often joke that I did not call the people in our church "lay-men" because they would take it as a command and just lay around. The dominant New Testament word for every believer is "saint," which means a holy one. Believers are all set apart to God for official, kingdom-oriented service. The apostles confidently put these men "in charge" (6:3 NASB) of this task with full assurance in the work of the Spirit in and through them for the good of the church. When the members of our churches sense our genuine confidence in the Spirit's work in and through them, the environment is marked by initiative, joy, and fruitfulness.

6. A Helpful Participation in Ministry

These seven were eager to take the administrative and operational burden off the apostles. I suggested to the men and women at the Titusville gathering that each of them ask their pastors, "What can I take charge of in our church to free you to focus on 'prayer and the ministry of the word'?" I believe this kind of movement of extraordinary leadership and service would transform the church and empower our pastors like never before.

This aspiration is reminiscent of the well-known story found in Exodus 17:8–16. Take a moment to read it with new eyes:

> Then Amalek came and fought with Israel at Rephidim. So
> Moses said to Joshua, "Choose for us men, and go out and fight
> with Amalek. Tomorrow I will stand on the top of the hill with
> the staff of God in my hand." So Joshua did as Moses told him,
> and fought with Amalek, while Moses, Aaron, and Hur went up
> to the top of the hill. Whenever Moses held up his hand, Israel

> prevailed, and whenever he lowered his hand, Amalek prevailed. But Moses' hands grew weary, so they took a stone and put it under him, and he sat on it, while Aaron and Hur held up his hands, one on one side, and the other on the other side. So his hands were steady until the going down of the sun. And Joshua overwhelmed Amalek and his people with the sword.

A group of desert raiders come against Israel. Moses summons Joshua to lead his first official battle. As we know, the strategic factor in this victory is Moses's visible dependence on God. The elevated "Rod of God" is reminiscent of the Lord's previous deliverances and would visibly encourage the troops. Moses's raised arms indicate a prayerful reliance on the power of God to win the day. The role of Aaron and Hur proves vital in the fight. When Moses's arms lower, the Israelite army falters in battle. When his arms are elevated, God supplies victory. Their support for Moses's prayerful leadership secures the victory perhaps as significantly as Joshua's military leadership.

In Their Own Words

Watch Pastor Malachi O'Brien describe a pastor's need for intercession at http://www.64fellowship.com/oldpaths/27/

It is not too much to say that Aaron and Hur were a picture of the influence of 6:3 saints who provide practical help to leaders who must remain devoted to "prayer and the ministry of the word." It is not too much to think that the prayers of church leaders will strengthen the young Joshuas of our ministry who are learning to trust God as they are on the front lines of battle.

The lasting significance of this Old Testament skirmish is captured in the description that follows: "Then the LORD said to Moses, 'Write this as a memorial in a book and recite it in the ears of Joshua, that I will utterly blot out the memory of Amalek from under heaven.' And Moses built an altar and called the name of it,

The LORD Is My Banner" (Ex. 17:14).

This was the first mention of the keeping of any official record about Israel's exploits. Significantly, it was a reminder of the role of prayer in their victories as a memorial for future engagements with their enemies. The great declaration was, "The Lord is my Banner" (Jehovah Nissi). As their trustworthy banner of victory, God, in His faithfulness, would bring them into future victories against their enemies.

7. A Holy Expectation of Supernatural Results

As we've already noted, the outcomes of this arrangement in Acts 6 spawned a powerful spiritual advancement; I've already described it as one of the greatest "revival" moments of the New Testament. "And the word of God continued to increase, and the number of the disciples multiplied greatly in Jerusalem, and a great many of the priests became obedient to the faith" (v. 7). No Christian is just filling a mundane spot of service in the church. God has called every believer to be a missional agent, just like the seven appointees in Acts 6:1–7. No matter how small the task, each is a vital part of Christ's great purposes of transforming the world with the Gospel.

MISSIONAL AGENTS WITHIN *YOUR* CHURCH

God uses men *and* women as servants within the church. *He has called every believer to be a missional agent*, just like the seven appointees in Acts 6:1–7. The subtitle of this book is "Awakening Your Church through Prayer and the Ministry of the Word." Old path shepherds facilitate a new experience of power in the lives of the saints.

Remember that praying pastors pave the way for an awakening of worship, leading to an awakening of witness and an awakening of workers as missional agents. This leads to an awakening of wonder at the power of Christ in the church and through the church in supernatural impact on a lost society.

In Their Own Words

Watch Pastor Troy Keaton (Eastlake Community Church, Moneta, VA) as he describes becoming a missional agent after a time of local crisis. See part one of two at http://www.64fellowship.com/oldpaths/28/. Then watch http://www.64fellowship.com/oldpaths/29/

Believe me friends, when the next revival comes, it will come as a surprise to everybody, and especially to those who have been trying to organize it. No revival that the Church has ever known has ever been an official movement.[1]

MARTYN LLOYD-JONES

How much will revival cost? Absolutely everything and absolutely nothing— that is how much it will cost. It will cost not one dime, and it will cost everything we have.[2]

A. W. TOZER

13

100,000 Points of Light

The early chapters of the book of Revelation picture the risen Christ walking gloriously among His churches. The apostle John, who during Jesus' earthly ministry was the "beloved" friend and participant in Christ's inner circle, was so overwhelmed with the magnificent vision of his triumphant, resurrected Savior that he fell to his face as though dead (1:17). In this holy encounter John saw:

> One like a son of man, clothed with a long robe and with a golden sash around his chest. The hairs of his head were white, like white wool, like snow. His eyes were like a flame of fire, his feet were like burnished bronze, refined in a furnace, and his voice was like the roar of many waters. In his right hand he held seven stars, from his mouth came a sharp two-edged sword, and his face was like the sun shining in full strength. (vv. 12–16)

Christ's opening words to John were, "Fear not, I am the first and the last, and the living one. I died, and behold I am alive forevermore, and I have the keys of Death and Hades" (vv. 17–18). The One who is the beginning and the ending of the human story is still triumphant, present, and life-imparting in and among His people. He still demands our full attention, worship, and obedience.

His messages to the seven churches in these early chapters of Revelation were varied in tone and substance. Yet our modern ears must be attuned to the relevance of His authoritative call to us today.

- Like the Christians in Ephesus, we must repent and be awakened to our first love for Jesus (2:1–7).
- Like the believers in Smyrna, we should see with new eyes the reality of future suffering and potential martyrdom, then embrace a faithfulness to death given our promised crown of life (2:8–11).
- Like the church in Pergamum, we must be aware of the work and wiles of Satan and rouse ourselves to reject the destructive deception of all forms of false teaching (2:12–17).
- Like believers at Thyatira, we must recognize, reject, and repent of all forms of sexual immorality and hold fast in purity until Christ returns (2:18).
- Like Christians at Sardis, we must be able to see when we have an appearance of life but are dead. We must answer the call to wake up and again strengthen the essential things of faith (3:1–6).
- Like Christ–followers in ancient Philadelphia, we must persist in genuine love, trusting our all-powerful Christ to bring his enemies into subjection, as we keep His Word in patient endurance (3:7–13).
- Like the Laodicean church, we must tune in to see our repulsive lukewarm condition and wake up to hear Christ knocking on the door, eager for a transforming reentry to His church (3:14–21).

We must be awakened, aroused, aware, and "Hear what the Spirit is saying to the churches." The living Christ still walks among His church, ready to bring them back to the fullness of His life.

⬈ In Their Own Words

Watch author and pastor John Franklin (John Franklin Ministries) speak honestly about "Revival and Responsibility" at http://www.64fellowship.com/oldpaths/30/

UNDERSTANDING REVIVAL

The old paths of best priorities and firm conviction create the environment for a new reality of the power of the Christ. Historically, we call this revival. Pastor Timothy Keller says a revival is "the intensification of the normal operations of the Holy Spirit through the ordinary means of grace."[3]

Martyn Lloyd-Jones wrote that revival is "a period of unusual blessing and activity in the life of the Christian Church. . . . Revival means awakening, stimulating the life, bringing it to the surface again."[4]

Del Fehsenfeld Jr., founder of Life Action Ministries, wrote that "Revival is the moving of God's Spirit, through the power of His Word, to the hearts of His children, that resurrects to new life those areas which have been lying stagnant, dormant, or out of balance, and that results in new love and obedience to Jesus Christ."[5]

Pastor and author Iain Murray gave this comprehensive clarification of revival:

> Revival is an outpouring of the Holy Spirit, brought about by the intercession of Christ, resulting in a new degree of life in the church and widespread movement of grace among the unconverted. It is an extraordinary communication of the Spirit of God, a superabundance of the Spirit's operations, and enlargement of his manifest power.[6]

Stephen Olford summarized with this definition, rooted in Christ's presence: "Revival is ultimately Christ Himself, seen, felt, heard, living, active, moving in and through His body on earth."[7]

How important is revival to the church? "The only eras of church history that are really worth studying with satisfaction are those periods when the church was in revival," writes Dr. Ed Hindson, dean of the Rawlings School of Divinity (Liberty University). He adds, "The highlights of the Christian church are its revival movements."[8]

REVIVAL VS. EVANGELISM

Lloyd-Jones pointed out that revival "happens primarily in the Church of God, and amongst believing people and it is only secondly something that affects those that are outside also."[9] He underscored the need to differentiate between revival and evangelism.

> To confuse these two things leads to much harm. There is nothing which is quite so foolish as people announcing that they are going to hold a revival. They mean an evangelistic campaign. An evangelistic campaign is the Church deciding to do something with respect to those who are outside. A revival is not the Church deciding to do something and doing it. It is something that is done to the church, something that happens to the Church.[10]

In our context, it is important to distinguish real, biblical revival from our scripted "movements," multimillion-dollar evangelistic happenings, and other large, aggressively promoted gatherings that we even call "revival" events.

Yet the fact remains that real revival will result in an astonishing impact on the lost. In Acts 6:1–7 the revived environment of the early church, led by the praying apostles, overflowed to extraordinary conversions, even among the Jewish priests (6:7). During the revival of 1857–58 that occurred through a movement of prayer begun by a Christian layman in New York City, *one million people were reported to become Christ-followers* from a population of thirty million in our nation.[11] That would be tantamount to 10.5 million conversions among the current U.S. population.

Professor Hindson observes, "Revival among the saved will always result in an outburst of evangelism among the lost. Evangelism is the automatic byproduct of revival. One may prod an unrevived congregation to soul-winning activity with gifts and gimmicks, but such prodding is unnecessary in the revived church."[12] J. I. Packer underscores this, "God revives his church and then the new life overflows from the church for the conversion of outsiders and the renovation of society."[13] As we see in the book of Acts, "For we cannot but speak of what we have seen and heard" (4:20).

ELEMENTS LEADING TO REVIVAL

Seek God, not Results

Imagine a genuine revival igniting even now as you are reading this sentence. A sovereign movement of the Word and Spirit sparks an awakening in our nation and beyond. The fervent prayers of an old path approach to leadership ushers in new power.

Now, imagine the scene twenty years later. The revival has subsided. The fruit of this awakening in the culture has transformed many elements of society. Things have changed for the better in astonishing fashion. Here is my question: Will we be praying with the same passion after the revival as we did before the revival? Hopefully the answer is yes. Our conclusion probably depends on the nature of our motivation. If the motive was only the desperate need for a touch from God, our prayers might have diminished.

There is difference between seeking revival from God and seeking God for revival. Seeking God for revival is rooted in a pure, passionate pursuit

The only enduring motive for prayer is that God is worthy to be sought.

of Him—nothing more, nothing less. As noted in an earlier chapter (and as I often remind myself), "The only enduring motive for prayer is that God is worthy to be sought." As Lloyd-Jones reiterates, "The inevitable and constant preliminary to revival has always been a thirst for God, a living thirst for a knowledge of the living God."[14]

A.W. Tozer captured this concern in these words:

> We make out that revival is everybody running around falling on everybody else's neck and saying, "Forgive me for thinking a bad thought about you. Forgive me for that nickel that I forgot to pay back." Or we say a revival consists of people getting very loud and noisy. Well, that might happen in a revival, but the only kind of revival that would be here when the worlds are on fire is the revival that begins by saying "Oh God, give me Thyself! For nothing less than Thee will do."[15]

Seek the Spirit in Us, Not around Us

The more I listen to modern worship songs that speak of the Holy Spirit as some impersonal force, hiding in the rafters, waiting for our invitation to appear in some magical fashion, the more concerned I become. Are we seeking a New Testament work, or some quasimystical understanding of His person and power?

A better New Testament truth emphasizes the Holy Spirit as the very presence of God living in us. He permanently indwells us as the proof of our salvation, teaching us, comforting us, guiding us, producing His character in us, and sealing us permanently until heaven appears.[16] Our desire in worship should be that the Holy Spirit would fill us as we surrender our hearts to His control.

When we describe or sing of the Spirit "falling" on us, it suggests some ethereal idea of hoping that the Holy Spirit will decide to suddenly do something outside us or around us, as if we are expecting some blue gas to appear in the atmosphere. Rather, we should pray that we become fully yielded, so the Spirit might be free to work powerfully in us for Christ's glory. As one professor said years ago, "The question is not how much of the Holy Spirit I have, but how much of me does the Holy Spirit have?"

Oh, how we need the Holy Spirit. But we need the real, New Testament, indwelling, empowering, enlivening work of the Spirit in our hearts as we fully surrender to the realities He describes about Himself in the Scriptures. When God sends true revival, He does it according to His Word. A bad pneumatology results in manipulated emotional substitutes that result in an ultimate setback of the true work of revival.[17]

The Power of Corporate Prayer

"There has never been a spiritual awakening in any country or locality that did not begin in united prayer," wrote A. T. Pierson.[18] In the 1860s, C. H. Spurgeon led prayer meetings at the Metropolitan Tabernacle. People met at 7 a.m. and 7:30 p.m. every day. One evening a visitor asked why Spurgeon's ministries were so successful. Spurgeon walked his visitor to the sanctuary, opened the door, and let him watch the participants praying that night. Nothing more needed to be said.[19]

Jonathan Edwards, the great Puritan preacher and educator, having witnessed the effects of the Great Awakening, wrote a now-famous treatise in defense of revival. He believed in the undeniable need for united prayer in view of an extraordinary work of the Spirit. The *shortened* title of the book reads, *A Humble Attempt to Promote Explicit Agreement and Visible Union of God's People in Extraordinary Prayer for the Revival of Religion and the Advancement of Christ's Kingdom on Earth, Pursuant to Scriptural Promises and Prophecies Concerning the Last Time.* Edwards understood and urged the reality that concerted, united, passionate prayer was always linked to revival. This is God's plan. As a result, this is one of the devil's primary strategies—to keep Christians from praying together.[20]

The Church, Not the Government

One of the great diversions today is the belief that electing a specific political party or redefining some social issue will bring real change to our nation. Please hear me. Christians should vote—always. We should graciously speak out on issues that concern us. But the United States and other nations are going downhill like an Olympic luge medalist because of one primary issue—the condition of human hearts. Hearts inform minds. Minds cast votes. Votes shape politics. Politics do not change the social landscape but rather reflect cultural realities. Only Jesus can transform hearts to reset the entire process.

Only the Gospel can change hearts, and changed hearts can change the world.

The governments of Jesus' and Paul's day were so pagan they make the American system look like a kindergarten recess. Yet nothing was mentioned about this evil state of affairs in any of the messages of Jesus or writings of Paul, except to say that we should pay our taxes and pray for our leaders. That is because Jesus and Paul knew that only the Gospel could change hearts, and changed hearts can change the world.

The great need of the day is for the church to pray for the church. Change starts among God's people. All other prayer targets are secondary and represent a superficial approach to the essence of revival. Two reminders underscore this essential focus. When Jesus commanded His followers, "Love your enemies and pray for those who persecute you," He did not indicate that any change would occur in the hearts of the enemies or persecutors. Note what He did say, "So that *you* may be sons of your Father who is in heaven" (Matt. 5:44–45, empasis added). He went on to reiterate, "You therefore must be perfect, as your heavenly Father is perfect" (v. 48). God's people change when they pray in the midst of a hostile culture.

When Paul prioritized the role of prayer in the church and went on to admonish believers to pray for "kings and all who are in high positions" (1 Tim. 2:1–2), he did not indicate that the policial leaders would suddenly have a spiritual epiphany. Rather he says, "that *we* may lead a peaceful and quiet life, godly and dignified in every way" (emphasis added). It is ludicrous to think that a changed government would produce these qualities in the lives of Christians. No. The work of prayer changes us to live these lifestyles that adorn the Gospel. This is the source of change in society. Paul underscores this in the following verses, indicating that our lives will please God, who "desires all people to be saved and to come to the knowledge of the truth" (1 Tim. 2:3–4). This only happens through the church.

Let's pray for all people, including the government and the enemies of the cross that are becoming more aggressive in our society and the world. But first let us pray for us. We are the salt of the earth and the light of the world. Transformation travels from the church into the world, not the other way around.

Indeed in a world darkened by sin, the redeemed people of God can serve as points of light. Such points of light can include an awakened and equipped pastor, a prayer mobilizer, or a church member who is committed to passionately and practically influence as many as possible. Those can seek God's face via Scripture-fed, Spirit-led, worship-based prayer, with the result that their church becomes a true "house of prayer for all nations," and an influence toward godly revival in our land.

Organic, Not Organizational

I have become convinced that the next revival among God's people, exploding into a culture-transforming awakening, will not come through megachurches or highly-publicized-event machinery. In our statistic-obsessed, media-crazed, self-promoting culture, the tendency toward self-exaltation is endemic. I sure feel the allure, and I assume you do as well.

Admittedly, we are all trying in some degree to grow our ministry and even expand our social media footprint. With the countless avenues available to us today, it would be very easy for highly visible, effectively organized prayer and revival endeavors to claim a piece of the credit for anything that looks, smells, or tastes like a work of the Spirit. For that reason, I believe that the next revival will be so organic that no one will be able to trace it to any highly touted human effort.

⌐⤢ In Their Own Words

Watch Pastor and Church Planter Jason Autry (Radius Church, West Columbia, SC) share his passion for "Revival Among a New Generation" at http://www.64fellowship.com/oldpaths/31/

"Organic" refers to something "arising as a natural outgrowth." I am praying for what we might call "100,000 points of light." It is a big dream. I am asking God to raise up 100,000 pastors of churches where the leaders have quietly and resolutely returned to the old paths. In faithfulness and obscurity they are doing what Christ has asked them to do. In obedience to the leadership of the Holy Spirit in their local context, they can lead each of their congregations to truly become a house of prayer for all nations. These 100,000 points of lights can shine the way for a revival in the hearts of congregations across America. I see this as the key to the next Great Awakening in our generation.

Os Guinness observes:

> Our much-needed reformation today will not come when
> Christian leaders sit around a board table with yellow pads and
> [outline] their vision from "mission" to "measurable outcomes."
> Rather it will come when men and women of God wrestle with

God as Jacob wrestled with the angel—wrestling with God
with their conscience, with their times, and with the state of the
church in their times, until out of that intense wrestling comes
an experience of God that is shattering, all-decisive and the
source of what may later once again be termed a reformation.
"I will not let you go unless you bless me."[21]

The goal is clearly not the elevation of any church, ministry, or personality—but that Christ would receive glory as congregations around the United States awaken to His presence and purposes. Worship-based prayer cultivates a deep repentance in His presence, a growing desperation for His power, and an unquenchable passion for His renown. J. D. Greear noted, "True revival is not noisy; at least, not at first. It usually begins in a hushed awe. Believers get convicted about sin and the seriousness of God's holiness. Weeping is heard before shouts."[22]

His Glory, Not Ours

The cry of Psalm 115:1 must shape our longing for revival, "Not to us, O Lord, not to us, but to your name give glory, for the sake of your steadfast love and your faithfulness!" I find it notable that "Not to us" is repeated twice. Our problem is seldom the desire to see God glorified. Rather, it is our tendency to want a bit of the glory for ourselves. I am continually convicted by God's pronouncement, "I am the Lord; that is my name; my glory I give to no other, nor my praise to carved idols" (Isa. 42:8).

We are beyond carved idols, but we have varieties of mechanisms in our promotional repertoire that compete with the glory of God. In our local churches, many components of our worship experiences come close to a modern carved idol. They are not chiseled with wood but technologically mind-blowing products sold in Silicon Valley, designed by Sony, manufactured by Microsoft, or promoted by way of high-tech projection. While none of these modern worship supplements are wrong, I doubt the Lord is going to bring revival in such a way that our gadgets get the glory.

Today it takes an astounding amount of discernment and intentionality for us to keep an "old paths" mindset, especially when the new paths pulsate with such titillating appeal. Yet we must relentlessly embrace the attitude of Paul when he wrote,

> For consider your calling, brothers: not many of you were wise according to worldly standards, not many were powerful, not many were of noble birth. But God chose what is foolish in the world to shame the wise; God chose what is weak in the world to shame the strong; God chose what is low and despised in the world, even things that are not, to bring to nothing things that are, so that no human being might boast in the presence of God. And because of him you are in Christ Jesus, who became to us wisdom from God, righteousness and sanctification and redemption, so that, as it is written, "Let the one who boasts, boast in the Lord." (1 Cor. 1:26–31)

All human boasting is an enemy of revival, in whatever subtle form it appears. The psalmist had it right when he wrote, "Will you not revive us again, that your people may rejoice in you?" Revival is marked by singular rejoicing in God, His power, His presence, His exploits, His renown, and the glory of His Gospel.

THE FINAL WORD
ON YOUR LIFE AND MINISTRY

As much as we all long for an extraordinary work of the Gospel and a coming awakening, there is a personal side to all of this. Our reward in heaven is directly linked to why we do what we do, how we do it, and for whom. The real scoreboard is in heaven. An Acts 6:4 approach to ministry is paramount to our reward in heaven and our reputation on earth.

Greear has written, "If everything you do is explainable by natural giftings, then at your funeral people will likely give you credit for your accomplishments. But if God is doing things through you that are 'impossible with men,' then at your funeral your friends are likely to give God the credit." Then he concludes, "The Spirit wants to glorify Jesus in your life, not you. Live today with your eulogy in mind, asking God to do through you what only he can get credit for. I want the summation of my life to be the words of Zechariah the prophet, ' "Not by might, nor by power, but by my Spirit" ' says the Lord" (Zech. 4:6).[23]

As Os Guinness has observed, "The church always goes forward best by going back first."[24] I believe the key to your Christ-honoring legacy is rooted in a turn for the better. A turn back—to the old paths of "prayer and the ministry of the word." A world-transforming work of the Gospel and the Spirit will not happen overnight, but we must believe that it can as we embrace the old paths. The sufficient Spirit is ready to meet us there with a new and transforming experience of His power.

Jonathan Edwards was perhaps the primary voice in the First Great Awakening, during eighteenth-century America. He noted that at the beginning, a few sermons were preached and some missions efforts were initiated, but a small number of converts were seen. "But then," Edwards notes, "God in so remarkable a manner took the work into his own hands and did as much in a day or two that, under normal circumstances took the entire Christian community, using every means at their disposal, with the blessing of God, more than a year to accomplish."[25]

May God unite our hearts in this prayer, "Oh God, take our work into Your hands. Eclipse our ordinary approach to ministry with a fresh display of Your extraordinary grace and power. And may we see it in our lifetime."

ON THE PATH TO POWER

A Dream for Organic Revival Among a New Generation
BY KYLE LANCE MARTIN

When a person hears the word "revival," many thoughts flood the mind. Perhaps *emotions*, *tents*, even *disorder*. True revival, however, is much more than a word imbued with emotion or traditional connotations. There is a dream being birthed in America—a dream for true, organic revival, stripped down of religion and characterized by a genuine love for Christ that leads to proclaiming Him to others.

Only God could orchestrate what we are beginning to see unfold across our nation. As our Time to Revive team travels from city to city, encouraging local churches and equipping believers to humbly seek after God and share the Gospel in unity, we have seen the acts of the Holy Spirit like never before. For example, in numerous cities across the state of Indiana, public schools excused students to go and pray with others, RV factory owners shut down their assembly lines so we could share the Good News in the middle of their workday, Chrysler and other national factories opened their doors to prayer and the Gospel. Meanwhile doctors invited us into their waiting rooms to pray with patients, and thousands of believers gathered to go out and share Jesus in their neighborhoods and towns.

After many years of seeking God for revival, we can honestly say that *revival is arising in Indiana.* No more hoping for it. No more thinking it can happen. What began as seven days of prayer in northern Indiana exploded into seven months of prayer and outreach throughout the state, and still continues to spread to neighboring cities and towns.

The dream that burns in my heart for revival is rooted in Acts 11:19–26, the record of how the church in Antioch was birthed through the obedience and faith of unnamed men. Organic revival in our day will follow the same biblical pattern seen in the work of the Holy Spirit to establish the early church.

Even as the early Christians were scattered, spreading the Good News as they went, today God is raising a remnant in the church, strategically placed throughout our nation and beyond (Acts 11:19). They have been perfectly positioned to impact their community and culture. As our team travels from city to city, calling the church together under the one banner of Jesus Christ, the remnant is rising up and leaving behind denominational, racial, generational, and socioeconomic barriers that used to divide. They are pursuing the kingdom of God and speaking the message of Christ in unity. When the church starts living and declaring the pure message of the Gospel in unity, a city and even a nation can be revived for His glory (John 17:23).

Our team's mission arose out of a simple, yet deep longing for revival amongst a group of no-names in Dallas, Texas. God furthered the early church through men of no prominence who were willing to follow the Holy Spirit and share the news that had changed their lives. Likewise, we are seeing Him birth something new through the obedience and faith of a group of nobodies willing to follow Him and devote our lives to furthering His kingdom.

God is awakening a string of no-named individuals to the truth of Jesus and how it transforms lives.

Organic revival will take place only upon the shoulders of men and women who are content to remain unknown, seeking glory for the Lord, not themselves, and keeping the Gospel at the center. God will not share His glory (Isa. 42:8). Just as the men of Cyprus and Cyrene in Acts 11—men without office in the church and whose identities are unknown—took the Gospel to the Gentiles of Antioch, accomplishing a great stride forward in the early church, so a true movement of God will be one of no names and no faces. Revival will elevate one Person and One alone—Jesus Christ.

As we deliver this good news, we must get back to the basics the first century message was founded upon. Believers are growing weary of the complicated messages that have come with the Gospel over the years. The legalistic messages are exhausting. Traditions have become elevated to the mystery of the message. Let's keep to the Gospel as Paul did—death, burial, and resurrection: "For I delivered to you as of first importance what I also received: that Christ died for our sins in accordance with the Scriptures, that He was buried, that He was raised on the third day in accordance with the Scriptures" (1 Cor. 15:3–4). No need to make this difficult to embrace.

Organic revival will happen only because the Lord's hand is with us in our pursuit (Acts 11:21a). A true movement of God cannot be manufactured or contrived. It will only come in the Lord's timing and in His way, and we will know it's happening because large numbers will turn to the Lord (Acts 11:21b).

When examining a movement of God for its integrity, we must ask, "Are people coming to know the Lord? Are disciples being made?" We aren't talking transfer of sheep—people moving from one congregation to another. We are actually talking about people *experiencing new life in Christ* (Acts 11:21, 24). And we're talking about people who become *disciples* of Christ, not just converts. The harvest is plentiful, we only need laborers willing to go out and ask God for the increase (Luke 10:2).

A movement of God will also draw seasoned believers and respected leaders who will begin to "come and see" (Acts 11:22). Jesus invited others to come and see, and so should we (John 1:35–46). There will be a time of testing and discerning what is taking place, and true revival will show itself pure. Faith leaders of yesterday will see what is happening and say, "That may not be how we have done things, but we see God's hand in it and we are jumping in!"

The fruit of the Holy Spirit will be the evidence of a true movement of God, just as it was of the men in Antioch and of Paul's work in spreading the Gospel (Gal. 2:8–9). For revival to spread, we must take the attitude of the early church pioneers who embraced God's ways (as evidenced by the fruit), even when they were unexpected or nontraditional. We must watch ourselves, that we are not falling into the attitude of the Pharisees who couldn't reconcile the new wineskin that Christ taught of with their self-conceived notions of what the Messiah's coming should look like. Ask the Holy Spirit if what is taking place is from Him. And when you see the grace of God, be glad, jump in, and leave behind all the hesitancies, questions, and what-ifs heaped upon us by centuries of tradition and ritual that have smothered the roots of our faith (Acts 11:23).

When a true movement of God takes place, people will want others to experience what they have seen. And those who have been touched by revival will come back to invest in the environment (Acts 11:25–26). And this newness of following Christ will be recognized as something separate, something different from the religious traditions our culture is accustomed to and comfortable with, just as the first believers in Antioch were set apart and given the new label "Christian."

We must get on our knees to pray for and pursue revival. Our nation needs it. We are desperate for a revival that is so purely of the Holy Spirit it breaks the mold of anything we have seen in our lifetime. It's time to revive who we are in Jesus Christ. True revival begins within us. Because when we embrace Him fully, the comfort zone we once put ourselves in goes away. There is no framework, and we are willing to follow the Holy Spirit wherever He leads, no longer concerned about pleasing man. It truly becomes walking by faith through the unknown. And that is when others will be drawn to Christ. They will want what we have.

He is coming quickly, and the time is now to awaken the world to His truth.

Kyle Lance Martin is the founder and chief executive officer of Time to Revive, an agency to share the Gospel and train disciples.

AN OLD PATHS PROFILE
PASTOR JON HOEKEMA

PASTOR JON HOEKEMA came to Horizon Community Church in Downers Grove, Illinois, in December 2003. After spending five years in sunny southern California, the winters of Chicago were just too hard to resist! The church website describes Jon as "passionate about prayer and seeking God's presence in prayer in his life, at Horizon, and in leading a prayer movement among congregations in the Chicago area through a regional coalition of Christian Reformed churches. He is also passionate about God's Word and making it relevant, real, and applicable to everyday life."

Yet Jon's passion for prayer was ignited only in recent years. After a ten-week sabbatical, Jon had a deep sense that something was missing in his ministry. After coming to a place of significant discouragement and desperation, he attended a one-day event with Jim Cymbala in Minneapolis, sponsored by The 6:4 Fellowship. As he describes it, he returned from that event "with a passion for prayer." He later attended other 6:4 events and subsequently participated in coaching groups designed to equip him in leading a culture of prayer.

Soon Jon brought his personal leadership to the weekly Wednesday evening prayer meetings; he also guided his leadership teams in extended time together in prayer. Jon regularly leads forty-five minutes of prayer before the Sunday morning services. Once a quarter he actually focuses the entire Sunday service on prayer.

Jon also has accepted invitations from other pastors who are hungry to experience a greater reality of prayer in their lives and churches. In recent years, Hoekema has served as the regional prayer leader for the Christian Reformed churches in the Chicago area. He has also led prayer sessions at the denomination's national meetings and spoken at their national prayer conference.

The wonderful part of Jon's story is that his church is small, and Jon is bi-vocational. Yet his passion and desire to serve his fellow pastors has given him favor in the region and across his denomination. God is ready to use humble pastors, who share His heart, in ways that modern ecclesiastical celebrities often disregard.

"As a pastor of a small church, I appreciate the role we can play in spiritual revival," Jon writes. "I think for far too long the broader church has had the attitude that the megachurches have it right and the small churches have to learn from them. It fit into the American success story. But the small church, and the medium size church, stand side-by-side with the large church for the kingdom. Each has a God-given part to play.

The church, no matter what size, when it is led by prayerful leaders, can be used by God for a great influence for which God called it to be."

In a recent post to his fellow denominational pastors, Jon wrote, "If we say we believe in the power of prayer, if we believe that God works through the prayers of his people, if we see that the Holy Spirit moved powerfully in response to the prayers of believers in the book of Acts and in the history of the church, then why does the church today not give a higher priority to prayer among the leadership of the church? Praying is the work of the church!" After several responses from his colleagues Jon elaborated, "I think that we have relied on our wisdom, on our power, on our emphasis of the Word and our understanding of it to the detriment to our relying on prayer. A prayerless church is a powerless church.

"And prayerless preaching is powerless preaching."

Pastors like Jon Hoekema play a vital role in the dream "100,000 points of light."

Afterword

A Hunger for Something More

Years ago dozens of pastors signed The 6:4 Fellowship charter, convinced that such a pastor-to-pastor connection would be one of the most important experiences possible for today's church leaders. They realized such a personal connection would not be the most attractive idea for those looking for quick-fix formulas, yet they believed it would awaken something fresh and essential in the hearts of pastors desiring a truly New Testament ministry. If pastors could not agree on the value of "prayer and the ministry of the word" for the sake of advancing the Gospel, then we truly had lost our understanding of biblical ministry.

But it takes more than agreement. Our interests must be more than a casual affirmation of these essential priorities. Too much is at stake right now for us to be content with anything less when it comes to our lifeline to the supernatural power of Christ. Ministers must devote ourselves to prayer and the ministry of the Word. This must occur individually for every pastor. But it must also become the focus of our leadership teams and the very environment of our churches.

In recent years, I have often joined Daniel Henderson with thousands of pastors in cities across our nation and have seen a growing hunger for something more. We have witnessed the deep need for regular encouragement. Daniel has desired to connect pastors to one another and provide resources that will provide daily encouragement. This is the heartbeat and hope of The 6:4 Fellowship. More importantly, this is the desire of the Savior we serve.

As you conclude your reading of this book, I urge you to let this be a new beginning. Visit www.64fellowship.com often. I recommend you join this fellowship so that you might receive regular encouragement; if you are part of the fellowship, tell others about the fellowship and the website with its resources. Connect with the other pastors in this vital community to learn from one another. Take advantage of all the training and events that are available to you and your leadership team.

Let's resolve to experience new power in the old paths of real, New Testament ministry. Then let us pray with expectation that Christ will work in ways we've never seen before in these difficult days in our society. The Gospel is still the power of God unto salvation, and Christ is sufficient for the work to which He has called us. So now, and until we finish this earthly race, let us passionately "devote ourselves to prayer and the ministry of the word."

JIM CYMBALA
Pastor, The Brooklyn Tabernacle

Notes

Introduction: Imagine!

1. J. D. Greear, *Jesus Continued: Why the Spirit Inside You Is Better than Jesus Beside You* (Grand Rapids: Zondervan, 2014), 203.

2. Os Guinness, *Renaissance: The Power of the Gospel However Dark the Times* (Downers Grove, IL: InterVarsity, 2014), 132.

3. John F. MacArthur, *The MacArthur Study Bible* (Nashville: Nelson, 2006), 1610.

4. Greear, *Jesus Continued*, 196.

5. Keeney Dickenson, *Prayer Life vs. Life of Prayer,* http://www.64fellowship.com/resources/articles/prayer-life-vs-life-of-prayer/

6. In 2009 Dickerson, then a reporter for the *Phoenix New Times*, received the Livingston Award for Young Journalists for his three-part series "The Doctor Is Out" on medical standards and regulation in Arizona; http://www.livawards.org/winners/past_winners.php?y=2009

7. "Southern Baptist Spending Crunch," *Christianity Today*, November 2015, 65; http://www.christianitytoday.com/ct/2015/november/southern-baptist-spending-crunch-imb-david-platt.html

8. Mariano Castillo and Kevin Conlon, "Kim Davis Stands Ground, but Same Sex Couple Gets Marriage License," 14 September 2015; http://www.cnn.com/2015/09/14/politics/kim-davis-same-sex-marriage-kentucky/

9. Susanna Kim, "Mozilla CEO Resigns after Protests from Gay Marriage Supporters," 3 April 2014; http://abcnews.go.com/Business/mozilla-ceo-resigns-calif-gay-marriage-ban-campaign/story?id=23181711

10. Nicholas Kristof, "A Little Respect for Dr. Foster," 29 March 2015; http://www.nytimes.com/2015/03/29/opinion/sunday/nicholas-kristof-a-little-respect-for-dr-foster.html

Chapter 1: Current Drift—Future Sift

1. Richard L. Mayhew, in *Rediscovering Pastoral Ministry: Shaping Contemporary Ministry with Biblical Mandates*, John MacArthur, ed. (Dallas: Word, 1995), 5.

2. Cited in Henry Blackaby and Claude King, *Fresh Encounter* (Nashville: Broadman and Holman, 1996), 83.

3. Bart D. Ehrman, *A Brief Introduction to the New Testament* (New York: Oxford Univ. Press, 2004), 313–14.

4. John Dickerson, *The Great Evangelical Recession* (Grand Rapids: Baker, 2013), 32.

5. "2015 Sees Sharp Rise in PostChristian Population, 10 August 2015; https://www.barna.org/barna-update/culture/728-america-more-post-christian-than-two-years-ago#.VjOf-suFNMt

6. Carol Pipes, "SBC Reports More Churches Serving Fewer People," Newsroom blog, 10 June 2015; http://blog.lifeway.com/newsroom/2015/06/10/sbc-reports-more-churches-serving-fewer-people/

7. "Southern Baptist Spending Crunch," *Christianity Today*, November 2015, 65; http://www.christianitytoday.com/ct/2015/november/southern-baptist-spending-crunch-imb-david-platt.html

8. Pipes, "SBC Reports More Churches."

9. "What Millennials Want When They Visit Church," 4 March 2015; https://www.barna.org/barna-update/millennials/711-what-millennials-want-when-they-visit-church#.VcNmfMvbL4g

10. David Murray, "Christophobia"; http://www.christianity.com/theology/christophobia-11674691.html

11. https://www.opendoorsusa.org/christian-persecution/

12. John F. MacArthur, "We Will Not Bow," sermon preached at Grace Community Church, Sun Valley, CA, 19 July 2015. Transcript available at www.gty.org/resources/sermons/80-425/we-will-not-bow.

13. http://dictionary.reference.com/browse/sift

14. A recent example is an educational accrediting agency investigating Gordon College (Wenham, Mass.) for forbidding homosexual practice for students and staff. See J. Paul Nyquist, *Prepare* (Chicago: Moody, 2015), 36.

15. Os Guinness, *Renaissance* (Downers Grove, IL: InterVarsity, 2014), 14.

16. G. K. Chesterton, *The Everlasting Man* (Garden City, NY: Image Books, 1955), 260.

Chapter 2: An Urgent "Leadership" Renovation

1. Os Guinness, *Renaissance* (Downers Grove, IL: InterVarsity, 2014), 14.

2. Warren Bennis and Burt Nanus, *Leaders; Strategies for Taking Charge* (New York: HarperCollins, 1997), 4.

3. Kenneth O. Gangel, *Feeding and Leading* (Wheaton: Victor, 1989), 31.

4. Abraham (Gen. 21:22), Isaac (Gen. 21:20; 26:3, 24, 28), Jacob (Gen. 28:15, 20; 31:3, 42), Joseph (Gen. 39:2, 21, 23; 48:21), Moses (Ex. 3:12; 33:15, 16; Josh. 1:17), Joshua (1:5; 17; 3:4; 4:4; 6:27; 7:12; 14:9), Gideon (Judg. 6:13, 16), Samson (Judg. 13:24; 14:6, 19; 15:14; 16:20), Samuel (1 Samuel 2:21; 3:19), Saul (1 Sam. 10:7), David (1 Sam. 16:13;, 17:37; 18:12, 14; 28; 20:13; 2 Sam. 5:10; 7:3; 1 Kings 1:37; 1 Chron. 11:9; 17:8; 2 Chron. 1:1), Solomon (1 Kings 1:37; 8:57; 1 Chron. 22:17; 28:20), Asa (2 Chron. 15:1, 9), Jehoshaphat (2 Chron. 17:3; 19:1, 9–11), Uzziah (2 Chron. 26:5), Hezekiah (2 Kings 18:7; 2 Chron. 31:21; 32:8), Ezra (Ezra 1:3; 8:18; 22, 31), Nehemiah (2:8,18, 4:20), Jeremiah (1:8), and Isaiah (41:10). In the New Testament see Luke 1:28 (Mary), 63–66 (John the Baptist), and Acts 11:21 (the disciples).

Chapter 3: Vision: Received or Achieved?

1. http://www.64fellowship.com/resources/articles/a-life-of-achieving-vs-receiving/

2. Peter Scazerro, *Emotionally Healthy Spirituality* (Nashville: Nelson, 2006), p. ??

3. John Piper, *Brothers, We Are Not Professionals* (Nashville: Broadman and Holman, 2002), 61.

4. Ibid.

5. Ibid.

6. As quoted by Walter Trobisch, *Martin Luther's Quiet Time* (Downers Grove, IL: InterVarsity, 1975), 4.

7. Deanna Marie Carr, "A Consideration of the Meaning of Prayer in the Life of Marin Luther," *Concordia Theological Monthly* 42, no. 10 (1971): 621.

8. *What Luther Says*, ed. Ewald M. Plass (St. Louis: Concordia Publishing, 1959), 1088.

9. See Matthew 11:25; John 11:41–42; John 12:27–28; John 17; Luke 22:31–32; Matthew 26:39, 42; Mark 14:36; Luke 22:42; Luke 23:34; Matthew 27:46; Mark 15:34; Luke 23:46.

10. J. D. Greear, *Jesus Continued: Why the Spirit Inside You Is Better than Jesus Beside You* (Grand Rapids: Zondervan, 2014), 210.

11. Jim Cymbala, *Storm* (Grand Rapids, Zondervan, 2014), 22–23.

12. Warren Bennis, *On Becoming a Leader* (Menlo Park, CA: Addison-Wesley, 1989), 77.

13. Henry and Richard Blackaby, *Spiritual Leadership* (Nashville: Broadman and Holman, 2001), 69.

14. Cymbala, *Storm*, 21.

15. Peter Scazerro, *Emotionally Healthy Spirituality* (Nashville: Nelson, 2006), 26.

16. Cymbala, *Storm*, 28.

Chapter 4: Overcoming Weapons of Mass Distraction

1. John Piper, *Brothers, We Are Not Professionals* (Nashville: Broadman and Holman, 2002), 59.

2. National Highway Traffic Safety Administration. "Key Facts and Statistics"; available from www.distraction.gov/stats-research-laws/facts-and-statistics.html. Based on 3,179 deaths involving distracted drivers in 2014.

3. http://www.usatoday.com/videos/news/2015/04/01/70791420/

4. John Piper, *Brothers*, 59.

5. Paul Vitello "Taking a Break from the Lord's Work," *New York Times*, 1 August 2010; http://www.nytimes.com/2010/08/02/nyregion/02burnout.html?_r=0

6. "Clergy Health Survey," June 2015, The Center for Health of the General Board of Pension and Health Benefits of The United Methodist Church; http://www.gbophb.org/assets/1/7/4785.pdf

7. Richard J. Krejcir, "Statistics on Pastors," originally published in 2007; http://www.intothyword.org/apps/articles/default.asp?articleid=36562

8. See http://www.churchleaders.com/pastors/pastor-articles/246531-3-hard-powerful-truths-likeability-leadership.html

9. Ernest Becker, *The Denial of Death* (New York: Free Press, 1977), 136.

10. Piper, *Brothers, We are Not Professionals,* 61.

11. C. H. Spurgeon, *Pray without Ceasing* (The Metropolitan Tabernacle Pulpit, vol. 18 (1872), from The C.H. Spurgeon Collection.

12. Quoted inWalter Trobisch, *Martin Luther's Quiet Time* (Downers Grove, IL: InterVarsity Press, 1975), 5.

13. H. G. Liddell, *A Lexicon: Abridged from Liddell and Scott's Greek-English Lexicon* (Oak Harbor, WA: Logos Research Systems, 1996), 401.

14. The books I used were J. Oswald Sanders, *Spiritual Leadership*; Donald Whitney, *Disciplines for The Christian Life*; Robert E. Coleman, *The Masterplan of Evangelism*; Ken Nair, *Discovering the Mind of a Woman*; and Daniel Henderson, *Fresh Encounters.*

Chapter 5: Finding the Conviction to Make a Change

1. Jim Cymbala, *Storm* (Grand Rapids: Zondervan, 2014), 138–39.

2. John Piper, *Brothers, We Are Not Professionals* (Nashville: Broadman and Holman, 2002),54.

3. Ed Stetzer and Thom S. Rainer, *Transformational Church* (Nashville: Broadman and Holman, 2010), 131.

4. Ibid.

5. http://store.brooklyntabernacle.org/products.php?product=My-House-Shall-Be-Called-A-House-Of-Prayer-(DVD)

6. For more information go to http://www.strategicrenewal.com/prayer coaching/

7. http://www.64fellowship.com/resources/sermons/tampa-rediscover-2012-session-1/

8. Martyn Lloyd-Jones, as quoted in Collin Hanson, *A God Sized Vision: Revival Stories that Stretch and Stir* (Grand Rapids: Zondervan, 2010), 14.

9. Ibid.

10. Daniel Henderson, *Fresh Encounters* (Colorado Springs: NavPress, 2004); and Daniel Henderson, *Transforming Prayer* (Grand Rapids: Bethany House, 2011).

Chapter 6: Leading a Powerful Culture of Prayer

1. Charles Bridges, *The Christian Ministry: with an Inquiry in the Causes of Its Inefficency,* 3rd ed. (London: Seeley and Burnside, 1830), 193.

2. E. M. Bounds, *The Complete Work of E. M. Bounds on Prayer* (Grand Rapids: Baker, 1990), 370–71.

3. Donald McDougall, *The Pastor's Prayer Life, John MacArthur and the Master's Seminary Faculty* (Dallas: Word, 1995), 184–85.

4. Ibid., 185.

5. Mark Vroegop, "Developing a Dynamic Prayer Culture in Your Church," 10 August 2014.

National 6:4 Fellowship Conference Workshops; http://www.64fellowship. com/resources/sermons/developing-a-dynamic-prayer-culture-in-your-church/

6. Daniel Henderson, *Fresh Encounters: Experiencing Transformation through United, Worship-Based Prayer* (Colorado Springs: NavPress, 2004).

7. For a powerful explanation of the priority of corporate prayer, read John Franklin, "5 Reasons Christians Must Pray Together," 20 November 2014; http://www.64fellowship.com/resources/articles/5-reasons-christians-must-pray-together/

8. Gene Getz, *Praying for One Another* (Wheaton, IL: Victor, 1983), 11.

9. C. H. Spurgeon, *The Metropolitan Tabernacle Pulpit*, vol. 19 (London: Passmore & Alabaster, 1873), 218.

10. John Piper, "Prayer: The Work of Missions," ACMC (Advancing Churches in Missions Commitment) Annual Meeting, Denver, 29 July 1988; http://www. desiringgod.org/messages/prayer-the-work-of-missions.

11. As quoted in https://www.biblegateway.com/devotionals/tozer-on-leadership/ 2015/09/02.

12. Al Toledo, keynote address, 2014 National Conference of Acts 6:4 Fellowship, Littleton, CO; 20 July 2014; http://www.64fellowship.com/resources/ sermons/al-toledo-keynote-2014/

13. Jim Cymbala, *Storm* (Grand Rapids: Zondervan, 2014), 37.

Chapter 7: How to Lead Life-Giving Prayer Times

1. C. H. Spurgeon, *Only a Prayer Meeting* (Ross-shire, Scotland: Christian Focus, 2000), 9.

2. George Mueller, as cited in Spurgeon, *Only A Prayer Meeting*, 154.

3. Daniel Henderson, *PRAYzing! Creative Prayer Experiences from A to Z* (Colorado Springs: NavPress, 2007), 21.

4. John Piper, "How to Pray for a Desolate Church," Desiring God Ministries, 5 January 1992, www.desiringgod.org.

5. George Müller, *Autobiography of George Müller* (repr. Denton, TX: Westminster Literature Resources, 2003), 153.

6. For an audio version of this entire training session on the eight principles for leading life-guiding prayer experiences, including the 4/4 pattern of prayer, go to http://www.64fellowship.com/resources/sermons/leading-life-giving-prayer-times; Daniel Henderson, "Leading Life-Giving Prayer Times" 10 August 2014, The 6:4 Fellowship National Conference, breakout session. (This is a fifty-one-minute session.)

7. Cliff Boone, "I Never Feel More Like a Pastor than When I Am . . ." 22 April 2015, "http://www.64fellowship.com/resources/articles/i-never-feel-more-like-a-pastor-than-when-i-am/

8. Boone describes his new understanding of prayer and in the priority of prayer ("prayer coaching") in a short video at /http://www.strategicrenewal.com/ prayercoaching

Chapter 8: A New Movement of Praying Churches

1. C. H. Spurgeon, *An All-Round Ministry* (Carlisle, PA: The Banner of Truth Trust, 1978), 313.

2. Sandy Mason, *Smarter than Jesus?* (Peoria, AZ: Intermedia Publishing Group, 2011), 45.

3. The covenant of The 6:4 Fellowship can be found at: http://www.64 fellowship.com/aboutus/covenant/

4. A. W. Tozer, *Tozer on Christian Leadership—A 366 Day Devotional compiled by Ron Eggert* (Camp Hill, PA: Christian Publications, 2001) April 2.

5. Manny Mill with Harold Smith and Barbara Mill, *Radical Prayer!* (Chicago: Moody, 2015), 30–31. Mill recounted that one conference speaker reported that "80 percent of evangelical pastors in America do not have a personal, private prayer life."

6. Jim Cymbala, *Storm* (Grand Rapids: Zondervan, 2014), 41.

7. Donald McDougall, "The Pastor's Prayer Life—*the Ministry Side*," ed. John MacArthur, *Rediscovering Pastoral Ministry* (Dallas: Word, 1995), 186.

8. We read and I recommend Alexander Strauch, *Biblical Eldership* (Dallas: Word, 1995; Gene Getz, *Elders and Leaders* (Chicago: Moody, 2003); and Jim Cymbala with Dean Merrill, *Fresh Wind, Fresh Fire* (Grand Rapids: Zondervan, 1993).

9. Watch the Hill Country elders share their story here: https://vimeo .com/53451824

10. See http://www.64fellowship.com/im-new/resources-in-your-region

11. Email from Jim Leggett, 21 October 2015.

12. For a glimpse of the Katy, Texas, story see "Monthly Feature: Praying Pastors of Katy, TX," 30 March 2012; http://www.64fellowship.com/resources/ articles/jim-leggett-part-1/

13. D. A. Carson, *A Call to Spiritual Reformation* (Grand Rapids: Baker, 1992), 35.

14. Matthew Henry, as quoted in Alvin L. Reid, *Join the Movement* (Grand Rapids: Kregel, 2007),142.

Chapter 9: Preaching with Understanding, Unction, and Utterance

1. D. Martyn Lloyd-Jones, *Preaching & Preachers* (Grand Rapids: Zondervan, 1971), 24.

2. E. M. Bounds, *The Complete Work of E. M. Bounds on Prayer* (Grand Rapids: Baker, 1990), 370.

3. Arturo G Azurdia III, *Spirit Empowered Preaching* (Ross-shire, Scotland: Christian Focus Publications, 2015), 86.

4. Johannes P. Louw and Eugene A. Nida, *Greek-English Lexicon of the New Testament Based on Semantic Domains*, vol. 1 (New York: United Bible Societies, 1989), 260.

5. Azurdia III, *Spirit Empowered Preaching*, 86.

6. John MacArthur, "Preaching," in *Rediscovering Pastoral Ministry*, ed. John MacArthur (Dallas: Word, 1995), 255.

7. Ibid., 255–56.

8. Ibid., 256.

9. *Luther's Works*, vol. 51, *Sermons I*, "Eight Sermons at Wittenberg, 1522," 77.

10. Bounds, *The Complete Work of E. M. Bounds on Prayer*, 370–477.

11. C. H. Spurgeon, *Lectures to My Students* (London: Passmore & Alabaster,1875; repr. Grand Rapids: Zondervan, 1954), 49.

12. Ibid., 50.

13. Azurdia III, *Spirit Empowered Preaching*, 14.

14. Spurgeon, *Lectures to My Students*, 50.

15. Azurdia, *Spirit Empowered Preaching*, 98.

16. Spurgeon, *Lectures to My Students,* 45.

17. Jim Cymbala, *Storm* (Grand Rapids: Zondervan, 2014), 134–35.

18. Geoffrey Thomas, "Powerful Preaching," *The Preacher and Preaching*, ed. Samuel Logan, Jr. (Philipsburg: Presbyterian and Reformed Publishing Company, 1986), 369.

Chapter 10: Men to Match the Message

1. Timothy Keller, *Preaching: Communicating Faith in an Age of Skepticism* (New York: Viking Press, 2015), 67.

2. Arthur Bennett, *The Valley of Vision: A Collection of Puritan Prayers & Devotions* (repr.; Carlisle, PA: Banner of Truth, 2014), 337.

3. Ibid., 340.

4. Carey Nieuwhof, "5 Character Tests Every Great Leader Passes"; http://www.churchleaders.com/pastors/pastor-articles/261329-5-character-tests-every-great-leader-passes.html

5. Thomas Watson, as cited by I. D. E. Thomas, *A Puritan Golden Treasury* (Carlisle, PA: Banner of Truth, 2000).

6. John Calvin, *Institutes of the Christin Religion,* book 1, chap. 1, trans. Henry Beveridge (Grand Rapids: Eerdmans, 1989), 38–39.

7. Ibid.

8. "Using Things and Loving People"; words by Archie Paul Jordan and Hal David; lyrics © Universal Music Publishing Group.

9. C. H. Spurgeon, *The Metropolitan Tabernacle Pulpit – Volume 17* (London: Passmore & Alabaster, 1871), 524.

10. F. F. Bruce, *The Epistle to the Galatians* (Grand Rapids: Eerdmans, 1982), 232–33.

11. Carey Nieuwhof, "When Do Leaders Cross from Honest Transparency to T-M-I?"; http://www.churchleaders.com/pastors/pastor-articles/172609-carey-nieuwhof-leaders-cross-from-honest-transparency-to-tmi.html

12. John MacArthur, "The Pastor's Study," *Rediscovering Pastoral Ministry,* ed. John MacArthur (Dallas: Word, 1995), 211.

13. Keller, *Preaching,* 205.

14. C. H. Spurgeon, *Lectures to My Students* (London: Passmore & Alabaster, 1875; repr. Grand Rapids: Zondervan, 1954), 47.

15. Spurgeon, "The Minister's Plea," *The Metropolitan Tabernacle Pulpit,* vol. 41 (London: Passmore & Alabaster, 1895), 518.

16. Spurgeon, *The Metropolitan Tabernacle Pulpit,* vol. 25 (London: Passmore & Alabaster, 1879), 695.

17. Keller, *Preaching,* 48.

Chapter 11: "God Is Truly Among You"

1. A. W. Tozer, "Beware the File Card Mentality," *Of God and Men* (Christian Publications, 1960; repr. Chicago: Moody, 2015), 83.

2. Arturo G. Azurdia III, *Spirit Empowered Preaching* (Ross-Shire, Scotland: Christian Focus Publications, 2015), 148.

3. "What People Experience in Churches," 8 January 2012; https://www.barna.org/congregations-articles/556-what-people-experience-in-churches#.VrQR9I-cHIU

4. "What Millennials Want When They Visit Churches," 4 March 2015; https://www.barna.org/barna-update/millennials/711-what-millennials-want-when-they-visit-church#.VsN0TuZTKsq

5. Ibid.

6. Jim Cymbala, *Storm* (Grand Rapids: Zondervan, 2014), 21.

7. This and other similar stories appear in Daniel Henderson, *PRAYzing! Creative Prayer Experiences from A to Z* (Colorado Springs: NavPress, 2004).

8. For even more radical ideas about what we might do to better facilitate a sense of the centrality and presence of Christ and the value of the church body in our services, see "If I Could, I Would: A New Old Way of Doing Church" at http://www.strategicrenewal.com/strategic-renewal-e--devotional/if-i-couldi-would/

9. Cymbala, *Storm,* 75.

10. A. W. Tozer, *Tozer on Christian Leadership—A 366 Day Devotional,* comp. Ron Eggert, July 20.

Chapter 12: A New Unleashing of Missional Agents

1. Ray C. Stedman, *Body Life* (Glendale, CA: Regal Books, 1972), 130.

2. Thom S. Rainer and Ed Stetzer, *Transformational Church* (Nashville: B & H Publishing, 2010), 3.

3. William Shakespeare, *King Richard the Second* Act I, sc 1, l. 177.

4. Francis Chan, with Danae Yankoski, *Forgotten God* (Colorado Springs: David C. Cook, 2009).

Chapter 13: 100,000 Points of Light

1. Martyn Lloyd-Jones, *Revival* (Wheaton, IL: Crossway, 1987), 166.

2. A. W. Tozer, *Tozer on Christian Leadership: A 366 Day Devotional,* comp. Ron Eggert (Camp Hill, PA: Christian Publications, 2001), September 11.

3. Timothy Keller, *Center Church* (Grand Rapids: Zondervan, 2012), 54.

4. Lloyd-Jones, *Revival*, 99.

5. https://lifeaction.org/blog/2013/1/1/january-2013-prayer-calendar/

6. Iain H. Murray, *Pentecost—Today? The Biblical Basis for Understanding Revival* (Carlisle, PA: Banner of Truth Trust, 1998), 23–24.

7. As quoted at http://deeperchristianquotes.com/stephen-olford-quote-on-revival/

8. Edward E. Hindson, *Glory in the Church: The Coming Revival* (Nashville: Nelson, 1975), 22.

9. Martyn Lloyd-Jones as quoted in Hindson, *Glory in the Church*, 99.

10. Ibid.

11. Ronnie W. Floyd, "Pleading with Southern Baptists," *SBC Life*, December 2014; http://www.sbclife.net/Articles/2014/12/sla8

12. Hindson, *Glory in the Church*, 21.

13. J. I. Packer, *Keep in Step with the Spirit* (Tarrytown, N.Y.: Revell, 1984), 256.

14. Collin Hansen and John Woodbridge, *A God-Sized Vision* (Grand Rapids: Zondervan, 2010), 15.

15. Tozer, *Tozer on Christian Leadership,* comp. Ron Eggert; September 13.

16. See John 14:7; Romans 8:14–16, 23, 26; 2 Corinthians 1:22; 5:5; Ephesians 1:13; 4:30, 5:18; and 1 John 4:13.

17. For more on the role of the Spirit in true worship, see http://www.strategicrenewal.com/strategic-renewal-e-devotional/spiritual-new-testament-worship/

18. As cited by J. Edwin Orr, https://renewaljournal.wordpress.com/nowhere/prayer-and-revival-by-j-edwin-orr/

19. Joel Beeke, "Prayer Meetings and Revival in the Church," in *Giving Ourselves to Prayer: An Acts 6:4 Primer for Ministry*, comp. Dan R. Crawford (Prayer-Shop Publishing, 2009), 305.

20. See "If I Were the Devil," http://www.strategicrenewal.com/strategic-renewal-e--devotional/if-i-were-the-devil/

21. Os Guinness, *Renaissance* (Downers Grove, IL: InterVarsity, 2014), 14.

22. J. D. Greear, *Jesus Continued: Why the Holy Spirit Inside You Is Better Than Jesus Beside You* (Grand Rapids: Zondervan, 2014), 201.

23. Ibid., 222.

24. Guinness, *Renaissance*, 132.

25. Jonathan Edwards, quoted in Collin Hansen, *A God-Sized Vision: Revival Stories That Stretch and Stir* (Grand Rapids: Zondervan, 2010), 179, revised in contemporary English.

Appendices

1. For more information about the Pastors In Covenant effort, watch https://www.youtube.com/ watch?v=iSEFtWg8YYc&safe=active2. http://www.strategicrenewal.com/strategic-renewal-e--devotional/false-advertising/

APPENDICES

Appendix 1

Eight Reasons Pastors Struggle to Lead in Prayer

As I speak in conferences and seminars, attendees frequently approach with pertinent questions during the breaks. Each inquirer comments up front on their genuine appreciation for their pastor. They typically extol their pastor's preaching, administrative skills, shepherding focus, and personality. Then they ask, "Why doesn't he lead our church in prayer?"

Feeling defensive of my colleagues yet wanting to give an adequate answer to these inquiries I have pondered the current realities that hold us back from true "old path" leadership priorities.

THE REASONS PASTORS STRUGGLE

In churches across the country today, congregations are desperate for a prayer movement. They look to their pastors for consistent example and passionate leadership. From my personal struggles as a pastor for almost thirty years, and through interactions with many peers, I have discovered eight basic reasons why pastors are reluctant to lead the way to a dynamic prayer ministry in the local church.

First, many grew up in a prayerless church environment. A Brazilian proverb states, "The heart cannot taste what the eyes have not seen." Today's pastors often lack the firsthand experience of functioning in a dynamic, prayer-energized church. Many pastors recall sparsely attended prayer meetings they've attended in the past. These prayer meetings involved prolonged grocery lists of physical needs and personal woes. A handful of faithful saints attended each week. However, a church where the majority of the people gather in dynamic, worship-based prayer does not register in the experience of most pastors' radar screens. It can be hard to lead something you've never experienced.

Second, most were trained in a prayerless educational process. I received seven years of formal undergraduate and graduate-level theological education. While grateful for all the fine classes and grand truths, I never had a professor or pastor personally influence me in the area of prayer. I heard great sermons on prayer and studied theological truths about prayer, but no one took me aside and taught me to pray by praying with me on a regular basis. Our formal academic preparation assumes that we understand prayer, and essentially diminishes its prominence. Accordingly, it does not play a prominent role in our approach to church ministry.

Third, some are not sure how to lead effective and life-changing prayer experiences. This lack of experience and training causes pastors to feel unsure and inadequate about the nature of life-giving prayer experiences. Since most received no training in the dynamics of leading biblical, balanced prayer gatherings, they struggle with the necessary confidence and conviction.

Fourth, all pastors minister in a prayerless, success-oriented culture. In many churches, being a "man of prayer" no longer ranks high on the list of desirable leadership traits for the local church. Instead, churches search for a manager or CEO (chief executive officer) type for the many programs and funding needs of the church.

This is the typical impact of living in a prayerless, success-oriented culture.

At one church leadership conference a man approached me after a session, identifying himself as the chairman of the pastoral search committee for a congregation in that area. He pulled out a list of more than eighty-five desirable attributes for their next pastor, compiled through a survey of the congregation. Many of the qualities centered on communication skills, management ability, pleasant personality, and strong pastoral-care interests. Nowhere on the list was there any mention of the priority of prayer as an essential for the new pastor.

Our American society tends to value strong, natural leadership, dynamic programming, entertaining services, and impressive technology. The idea of a pastor locked away in extended prayer does not strike the average churchgoer as a mark of effective leadership.

Fifth, many pastors want to avoid the embarrassment of a prayerless church. Pastors often sense a fresh motivation to call the church to pray collectively in some fashion. Unfortunately, the participation can be very low. In a day when most church efforts are evaluated by the numbers, pastors feel embarrassed by the poor turnout; so they decide to abort the effort rather than face the embarrassment of a sparse crowd. The pastor's hope is that people will just maintain a dynamic and consistent personal prayer life. Most often, they don't.

Sixth, some battle a prayerless personal life. It's difficult to take the church farther than you have journeyed in your life. This sense of failure and guilt immobilizes many pastors in the church prayer ministry. Satan, the "accuser of our brethren," works overtime to condemn and demoralize. Of course, the best way to shut down these accusations is to just start leading the people of the church in prayer. The pastor will pray more and the people will pray more. It is a win-win.

Seventh, others secretly question the efficacy of prayer. Some have not seen answers to prayer in the past and therefore are reticent to "go to the mat" in leading the people. This lack of faith is often rooted in a failure to recognize that "unanswered prayer" often brings a greater grace. (See Paul's commentary in 2 Cor. 12:7–10.) A new resolve must be rooted in a strong conviction about God's goodness and sovereignty in responding to the cries of His people. Beyond this, He is always worthy to be sought, regardless of our limited perspective on how He is responding to our expectations in prayer.

Finally, every pastor is a special target of the enemy. The enemy works overtime to divert, discourage, and derail well-meaning church leaders at every turn. It has been said that if the devil cannot make us bad, he will just make us busy. As long as the pastors do not tap into the supernatural work of prayer, the church will be content to engage in a nice, socially pleasing ministry, but will have little Spirit-empowered impact.

HOW SHOULD WE RESPOND?

These eight observations are not intended as cause for condemnation, but can serve as prompters to new resolve. They can provide greater understanding and support for pastoral colleagues who are struggling. With this awareness, we can identify the obstacles and pray for new Spirit-imparted resolve to press on in leading into new horizons of spiritual power as we continue earnestly in prayer.

APPENDIX 2

The Pride Divide: How the Devil Undermines Prayer

There was a time I believed every church member would automatically and wholeheartedly embrace the call to prayer and that more prayer would always bring more blessings. Today, I have learned otherwise.

The culprit that has spoiled my expectations is pride. I call it "the pride divide." Because the enemy is always counterattacking any renewed emphasis on prayer, the insipid infection of pride can infiltrate the hearts of both those who embrace the initiative and those who do not.

I have learned that when a pastor and congregation get serious about prayer, they pick a fight with the devil at a whole new level. Our enemy's tactics are subtle, serious, and often divisive.

Pride is described as "the snare of the devil" (1 Tim. 3:6–7 NASB). The snare makes its way into the prayer movement in such subtle fashion it is hardly noticeable until the symptoms show up in serious conflict. Pride is like bad breath—everyone but you knows you have it. This snare needs to be identified, exposed, and addressed to prevent its destructive power from undermining God's plan for a praying church.

Two camps can easily emerge to oppose prayer in the church. The first group I call the "resenters"; the second, the "resisters." No one really plans to join either camp, but the signs of subtle pride are obvious once they occur.

CAMP ONE: THE RESENTERS

The "resenters" can surface among those who jump wholeheartedly into the prayer ministry. Those who relish their new experiences share the blessings of prayer with great enthusiasm. Because prayer is something that must be experienced and can seldom be adequately explained, others who aren't as involved don't share the excitement. This lack of participation can be interpreted as a lack of spirituality—or a failure to support the leadership of the church. Soon the prayer-energized saints begin to resent the nonparticipants, feeling they are carnal.

Without great care and sensitivity, a pharisaical-like pride can begin to surface. While the real fruit of prayer should be seen in humility and grace, the snare is always present. This can create an equal and opposite reaction, the rising of the resisters.

CAMP TWO: THE RESISTERS

Soon, the roots of pride can grow deep in the soil of a different group. I call them the "resisters." Non-participants begin to dig in their heels and even become antagonistic to the new initiatives. Typically, they are reacting more to the overbearing zeal of the enthusiasts than to the actual call to prayer.

Of course, some Christians do not sense a need for a deeper walk with Christ. Their flesh can push back when they see others growing in a deeper enthusiasm. Self-satisfaction and an unwillingness to expand their prayer experience can be symptoms of stubborn flesh—but not always.

DECONSTRUCTING THE PRIDE DIVIDE

So what is a church to do once the pride divide has reared its ugly head? In my years of prayer leadership as a pastor, the following lessons have helped break down the "pride divide" and keep everyone focused on the right goals.

1. Honesty is the best policy.

Church leaders must acknowledge the divide, or at least the potential of it, and determine to address it openly with understanding and grace. Several times over the years, I have spoken from the pulpit on a Sunday morning of this dilemma. I have noted the devil's desire to undermine prayer and unity in the congregation. Just the act of exposing this danger allows people to talk about it, recognize it, and find greater resolve to avoid it. It also serves public notice on the forces of darkness that we are all alert to their schemes.

2. Understanding goes a long way.

It is helpful for the "resenters" to remember that just because someone cannot participate in the prayer programs does not mean they are less committed to seeking the Lord. The "holdouts" may have a variety of legitimate reasons for not participating in the call to united prayer. Simple issues like scheduling conflicts, job responsibilities, or health concerns may prevent them from plugging into the programs as they would like. Of course, some hold back due to fear, intimidation, or ignorance. Ultimately, it is the Lord's place, not ours, to judge their motives. Not all non-participation is motivated by pride.

As a leader, it is important to remind people that "the LORD does not see as man sees; for man looks on the outward appearance, but the LORD looks at the heart" (1 Sam. 16:7 NKJV). It is good to explain to the "resenters" that public prayer activity is not the only gauge of spiritual authenticity. "Resisters" need to be reminded that the extreme outward zeal of the prayer adopters often reflects a very sincere and seeking heart, for which we should always be grateful.

3. Prayer is intimacy, not activity.

As prayer ministry develops, it is easy to get wrapped up in the activity of prayer and lose the focus on the core issue of relationship with God. This is really the contrast we see between the prayer approach of the Pharisees and that of Jesus. In His Sermon on the Mount, Jesus reprimanded the Pharisees for reducing prayer to a public display of religious superiority. In contrast, He told His followers to humbly gather in a secret place to experience intimacy with their Father in heaven (Matt. 6:9–13). Similarly, we can fall into the trap of making prayer a "program for God" rather than the pure and simple pursuit of His person and presence.

The program mentality is fertile soil for the weeds of pride. Prayer leaders must emphasize the difference between a prayer program, which is focused on activities and numbers, and a prayer culture, which is about people praying in a variety of equally legitimate forms.

4. Only the Holy Spirit can motivate people to pray.

Ultimately, only the Holy Spirit can draw people into a deeper commitment to prayer. Any other pressure can become polluted with guilt, intimidation, and carnal obligation. If Jesus wants His church to be a house of prayer, His Spirit is able to make it so. Each of us must find our place in this plan, and graciously pray that others will do the same. This environment of humility and grace makes it difficult for the "pride divide" to thrive for very long.

"Resenters" should regularly place their trust in the Holy Spirit rather than announcements and recruitment efforts to motivate others to pray. This takes the pressure off human efforts to push things forward. Instead, we must trust the Holy Spirit and ask Him to do His work, in His way, to call His church to prayer.

"Resisters" should be encouraged to listen not to the voice of prayer enthusiasts but to the voice of the Holy Spirit. That still small voice is the ultimate invitation to intimacy with God and is fully sufficient to defuse pride and build a house of prayer.

GRACE FOR THE PRIDE DIVIDE

First Peter 5:5–6 reminds us, "Clothe yourselves, all of you, with humility toward one another, for 'God opposes the proud but gives grace to the humble.' Humble yourselves under the mighty hand of God, that He may exalt you in due time."

Real humility works in concert with honesty, understanding, intimacy with Christ, and a focus on the power of the Holy Spirit. This humility invites grace and allows us to express mutual submission. "Resenters" can trust Christ for the grace that will draw others into prayer. "Resisters" can receive the grace that will lead them into prayer. Together, they will be exalted to a higher level of spiritual understanding and intimacy as they learn to seek the Lord on the common ground of humility.

APPENDIX 3

Why Elders Matter

I n ministries across the land, a variety of terms are used to describe the spiritual leaders of congregations. In my journey, I have always served with "elders" who were the primary spiritual overseers of the church. Most of us see the names of our congregational leaders in the Sunday bulletin or on the church website but we seldom think of the profound effect they have on the life of the church (and our own spiritual journey) through their function and focus.

In my travels, I have found that congregational "elders" serve in a variety of roles. In some churches they do all the preaching on a volunteer basis. In other churches, they are business advisors for the staff, selected for their financial acumen or corporate success, functioning more like trustees than spiritual leaders. Sometimes they are just a group of supporters for the pastor and his plans, with no real spiritual authority. It seems the term cries out for definition in many churches.

WHO AND WHAT ARE "ELDERS"?

The title of "elder" comes from the New Testament Greek word *presbuterous,* which refers to the spiritual maturity required of those who lead the church. The New Testament always refers to elders in the plural, indicating a team of godly leaders. They are required to live exemplary lives (1 Tim. 3:1–7; Titus 1:6–9), teach God's Word (1 Tim. 3:2; Titus 1:9–11, 2:1; 2:7–8), and give spiritual leadership to the church (Acts 20:28; 1 Tim. 5:17–18). They are held to a higher standard and are accountable to God for the well-being of the congregation (James 3:1; 1 Tim. 5:19; Heb. 13:17).

Effective elders are worthy of honor. Some are worthy of "double honor," implying that some are paid by the church based on their responsibilities while others serve voluntarily (1 Tim. 5:17–18).

ELDER, PASTOR, OR BISHOP?

Many believers wonder about the difference in the various terms churches use to describe their leaders. The most definitive passage is found in Acts 20:17–38, where Paul addressed the leaders he had developed at the church of Ephesus in the span of his three-year ministry there. He used three different titles in speaking to these men. First, he called them "elders" (*presbuterous*) in verse 17. He then called them "overseers" in verse 28 (*episkopos*). This is the term that we use for "bishop." Finally, he described them as "shepherds" (*poimen*, v. 28 NIV). This is the term used for pastor.

So, these were not three separate roles, but different descriptions of the same group of leaders. The word *elder* refers to their spiritual maturity. *Bishop* describes their spiritual authority. *Pastor* is the description for their spiritual function.

ELDERS VS. APOSTLES?

The church began in Acts with apostles in the primary leadership role. The book of Acts concludes, and the other New Testament letters are written, with the elders in the leadership role. When did this transition occur? In Acts 15, we see the church in Jerusalem dealing with the difficult issues of Old Testament law and its ramifications on the message of the grace of the Gospel. In this deliberation, we see the apostles (personally chosen by Christ, personal witnesses of His resurrection, and commissioned to lay the foundation of the church through their teachings) working in concert with "elders" (Acts 15:2, 4, 22–23). After this, the focus of spiritual leadership shifts to the elders (bishops and pastors) as the leadership team of the churches across the region.

ROOTS MATTER

We have already seen that elders lead and feed the church with the truth while meeting the qualifications outlined in the New Testament. However, what priorities must they embrace to lead effectively? In tracing the actual function of the spiritual leaders of the church, it is important to go just a bit earlier in the Acts account. This brings us to Acts 6:1–7, where the apostles were coping with an operational breakdown in the all-important widow-feeding effort. Rather than becoming absorbed in managing this crisis, they appointed seven other godly, wise, Spirit-filled men to completely handle this task. (This group was the first example of what would eventually emerge as the "deacon" function.)

The clear, functional priorities of these apostles were "prayer and the ministry of the word." Through these primary priorities they kept the spiritual integrity of the leadership intact as they collectively received direction from the Spirit while guiding the church in biblical truth. The result was the blessing of God in supernatural power and Gospel expansion (see Acts 6:7). This focus also forced them to empower other leaders to direct vital ministries. This forms an important model for modern-day elders, pastors, and bishops rooted in the indisputable function of the apostles.

Why do the focus and function of elders matter so much? Simply put, a diluted focus among the leaders results in diminished spiritual vitality and derailed impact throughout the church. Secular models, biblical confusion, the demands of people, and the "distraction tactics" of the devil all converge to get elders off task. The church falters and the mission is weakened. I believe it is imperative that modern-day elders maintain a relentless commitment to "prayer and the ministry of the word" while empowering others to handle the many operational, financial, and programmatic functions of the church (whether through paid staff or trained volunteers). The supernatural advancement of the mission of Christ depends on it.

FIVE PRACTICAL APPLICATIONS

So, in the practical reality of today's congregational life, what can the elders do? Our leadership team embraced five key priorities:

1. *Dependence.* A collective commitment to seek the Lord through extraordinary prayer and to lead the church to become a house of prayer through our example.
2. *Doctrine.* A collective resolve to study God's Word and engage in individual teaching of the Scriptures to ensure doctrinal purity and practical equipping.
3. *Direction.* A collective responsibility to discern the direction of the Holy Spirit and guide the church toward His plans for the ministry.
4. *Discipline.* A willingness to become engaged in the final stages of the process of spiritual restoration of believers caught in sin (outlined in Matt. 18:15–20).
5. *Deployment.* A commitment to constantly "equip the saints" to do the work of the ministry of the church for the building up of the body of Christ (Eph. 4:11–12).

APPENDIX 4

The Delight and Danger of Pastors Praying Together

Pastors are a unique breed with a high calling and dangerous pitfalls. Strategic targets, they must be on constant guard against the wiles of the devil. Our enemy's ploys seem to be most effective when a pastor becomes isolated from life-giving, transparent connection with other leaders.

For decades, I enjoyed the privilege of praying with fellow pastors on a regular basis. While I seldom "had" time to do this, I felt convicted to "make" time. Not only did this regular fellowship enrich my soul, but it consistently lifted my perspective to a new place of concern for God's kingdom, and beyond the snare of personal and ministry myopia.

THE DELIGHTS

The delights of praying with other pastors are numerous:

1. *Understanding and Support.* The pastoral vocation is unique. Finding others who can commiserate with genuine insight and prayerful support is difficult. While it takes time to build trust and authentic confidentiality, mutually caring pastoral friendships and prayer connections can offer a safe place for leaders to carry one another's burdens.

One example is a "Pastors in Covenant"[1] group, designed to allow pastors to meet monthly in a smaller group for sharing and prayer. Pastor Hawks of Hill Country Bible Church (Austin, Texas) describes his involvement in the Pastors in Covenant group as one of the most revolutionary things he has done for his own soul, noting that these men have become his best friends.

2. *Growing in Faith.* Beyond the encouragement and prayer support, Hawks highlights a vital, but surprising benefit. He notes, "Prayer gives you an intimacy with God, but also with others' experience with God, that leads to a deeper understanding of who God is." Hawks speaks openly of his performance-oriented upbringing and how it misshaped his view of God. He describes the power of hearing another pastor speaking in worshipful prayer of the unconditional love and pleasure of God in His children. This affected Hawks deeply in this walk with Christ.

3. *Kingdom Impact.* When pastors pray together, seeking God's heart and will, it is very common that the Lord will impart a bigger concern to the hearts of these pastors. Soon they realize that no single church is effective enough to reach the entire community for the Gospel. Churches learn that they can do more together than apart and typically will discover the Lord's unique plan for increased Gospel impact.

4. *The Blessing of Unity.* Every father knows the heartache that comes when his children fight or are estranged from one another. The Heavenly Father grieves when the body of Christ is fragmented, combative, and openly behaving in a way that discredits the Gospel. Not only is there blessing in a genuine prayerful unity (Psalm 133), but the testimony of the church in the community is strengthened.

THE DANGERS

There are also some dangers that emerge when pastors embrace a commitment to pray together:

1. *Neglecting the Home Front.* After many years of praying consistently with other pastors I heard a statement that convicted me. "If it doesn't work at home, don't export it." I realized that it was a contradiction to be promoting prayer among the pastors at a citywide level if I was not leading my own church to become a house of prayer. Both are important, but it seems to me that trying to mobilize prayer among pastors who are not leading their own churches in significant prayer is a bit of a contradiction.

2. *False Advertising.* In one of my weekly devotionals I expressed my concern about false advertising as it relates to our promotion of prayer gatherings in the church. We announce a prayer meeting that is really a Bible study, a discussion time, and even an extended season of talking about prayer needs, but includes very little real, biblical prayer. When pastors' "prayer groups" involve mostly small talk about current events, commentary on their attendance figures, and long discussions about secondary ministry issues, they should not be classified as prayer. It is important that prayer gatherings get right to the business of extraordinary prayer as quickly as possible.

3. *Diluting the Gospel.* The purpose of all prayer is to discover the heart and provision of God for the advancement of His Gospel mission. While interdenominational relationships can be highly encouraging, it is imperative to guard the common core of the Gospel. Pastors can disagree on Calvinism, Arminianism, the end times, church polity,

modes of baptism, and spiritual gifts—and still pray together. But without a firm agreement on the core essential of the Gospel, the effort can downgrade to a milquetoast social coalition that will not produce any ultimate mission-relevant impact. It is wise for pastors to agree on this early on as they seek God's face and then join in His redemptive purposes in the community.

APPENDIX 5

Blended, Biblical, Beautiful Worship

All my life, worship services have seemed basically the same. Of course, some of the stylistic elements have changed. Hymnbooks have been replaced with the words for modern songs on a screen. Organs have almost disappeared, while electronic synthesizers and guitars have taken center stage. In many churches large wooden pulpits have given way to smaller stands—or no podium at all.

In spite of these changes, not much has really changed in the elements of the vast majority of worship services. What do I mean? The essential components are the same, usually in the same order: singing, then preaching, with occasional prayer and announcements sprinkled in. The service is neatly segmented between worship in music and worship in the Word. Prayer is typically a seasoning on the meat and potatoes of the gathering.

WHY SO SEGMENTED?

Who says it has to be this way? Why must we segment and subdivide the services into these distinct compartments? Here is a radical, maybe not-so-crazy proposal that might change how we worship on Sundays.

Instead of twenty minutes of music followed by forty minutes of preaching, zipped up neatly with an opening and closing prayer, imagine if the service looked more like this:

- Worship in song (8 minutes)
- First preaching segment (12 min.)
- Praying together about what we have just heard (5 min.)
- Short song of worship (3 min.)
- Second teaching segment (15 min.)
- Praying together about what we have just heard (5 min.)
- Short worship song (3 min.)
- Third teaching segment (10 min.)
- Praying together about what we have just heard (5 min.)
- Worship & response (7 min.)
- Worship through giving/ministry announcements (5 min.)
- Final worship (3 min.)

OBJECTIONS?

One immediate objection some may raise is that shorter teaching segments represent some kind of compromise of the Scriptures. Of course, the Bible is clear that we must accurately teach and passionately preach God's inspired Word. However, the Bible attaches no time requirements related to the delivery of the message. In fact, if you read and timed some of the sermons of the New Testament, you would find that they are shorter and more effective than most sermons in our churches today (Acts 2:4–41; 4:8–12; 7:2–53). An exception might be Paul's teaching on the Lord's Day in Troas when he spoke late into the night and Eutychus dozed off, and then fell from the upstairs window (Acts 20:7–12). The point remains that effective preaching is not necessarily attached to a certain timeframe.

BENEFITS OF INTEGRATION

I see several benefits to this kind of approach.

1. Attention

Like it or not, the attention span of Americans is getting shorter. Research is even showing that with all of the technological multi-tasking we practice via smartphones, iPads, and email, our brains are actually being remapped, making activities that require extended focus more difficult. I don't necessarily like this and believe it has ramifications on our spiritual health. But it is what it is.

Shorter components, punctuated with prayerful application and worship, might encourage better focus and engagement. That is a noble goal for every gathering. I remember attending a church where the sermons were typically fifty-five to sixty-five minutes. Few people could even remember what was said at the beginning of the sermon after fifty minutes had elapsed. I noticed a lot of dozing going on, even amid the attempt to take notes. Content overload might lead to a full head, but not necessarily an engaged will. (For those who are keeping count, the three proposed preaching/teaching segments total thirty-seven minutes.)

2. Interaction

We have become a spectator culture when it comes to worship. Even when we sing we give our attention to the performers on the platform. We passively listen to extended messages with very little crowd participation.

Taking time to pray and worship in connection with shorter segments of teaching and response causes our minds and hearts to engage in the power of God's Word. Contextually appropriate expressions of prayer give attendees the opportunity to connect with one another at a meaningful level. This could include private prayer, small group prayer, prayer led from the front, and other formats.

3. Application

Recently, the senior pastor at a church I am working with commented, "I've become convinced that the most powerful way to apply God's Word is to pray it." I agree. Even the opportunity to sing thematically related songs in connection with a teaching segment can become a uniting and inspiring way to engage with the truth as a worshiping community.

The goal of our teaching is to engage the mind and heart in order to affect the will. This leads to a deeper application and obedience. The goal of our singing is to employ the entire being in extolling the character of God with a keen awareness of His presence. Substantive prayer, woven into the service, enhances all of these goals.

4. Spirit and Truth

In John 4:24 Jesus gave the landmark statement on worship, declaring that the Father is seeking those who will worship Him "in spirit and truth." His words remind us that we should pursue a balance of heart and mind, interaction and information, commitment and content. Perhaps a more intentional and interactive integration of both elements would produce an experience that would aid our journey toward Christlikeness and mission engagement.

HOLY DISSATISFACTION?

Admittedly, a change of this sort might "upset the apple cart." Candidly, many believers want a predictable, comfortable, and heady experience. It is very likely that a more interactive experience would be threatening to some who are completely satisfied with the status quo. However, the boldness to try something more engaging might be worth the experiment.

Who knows, maybe a different approach would produce a different result. A different result might shape a different kind of disciple, leading to a different kind of impact on people who so desperately needs to encounter passionate, pure, and powerful believers walking in the light of the Gospel of Jesus Christ.

Also by
Daniel Henderson

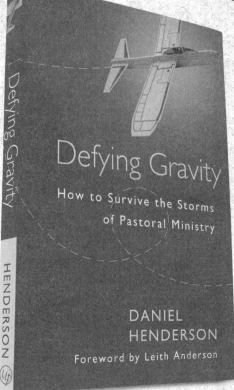

ISBN: 978-0-8024-0952-2

Defying Gravity makes leaders aware of the pitfalls of ministry and equips them with the tools to avoid these temptations and traps by monitoring nine gauges on the "leadership instrument panel." If you can learn to rely on these instruments, you too can keep your ministry soaring no matter what storms come your way!

also available as an ebook

MOODY
Publishers™

From the Word to Life